D R Toi
223 Southlake Pl
Newport News VA 23602-8323

4-14-2010 Ritz VA/DC
read all in 3-4 hours

10-10-10

10 Minutes, 10 Months, 10 Years

•

A Life-Transforming Idea

Suzy Welch

SCRIBNER

New York London Toronto Sydney

SCRIBNER
A Division of Simon & Schuster, Inc.
1230 Avenue of the Americas
New York, NY 10020

Text set in Granjon

Manufactured in the United States of America

ISBN-13: 978-1-4165-9182-5
ISBN-10: 1-4165-9182-6

Certain names and identifying characteristics have been changed and certain individuals are composites.

With love, respect, and gratitude,

I dedicate this book to the 10-10-10ers who shared

their stories of transformation

Contents

Introduction: Before Sunrise 1

1. It Was What?
10-10-10 in the Light of Day 9

2. This Is Your Brain on 10-10-10
The Science Behind the System 31

3. Authentic at Last
The Values Equation of 10-10-10 53

4. Happily Ever After
10-10-10 and the Code of Love 71

5. In Work, Dignity
On the Job with 10-10-10 99

6. You Can Get There from Here
Charting Your Career with 10-10-10 123

7. Teach Your Children Well
10-10-10 as Your Partner in Parenting 149

8. Lean on Me
Friendship Lost and Found with 10-10-10 173

9. The Mistletoe Dart
Some Thoughts on 10-10-10 and the Circle of Life 195

Conclusion: The Happiness List 217

Acknowledgments 223

10-10-10

INTRODUCTION

Before Sunrise

I was born in Portland, Oregon—*exotic* Portland, as I like to say, since it always seems to get a laugh. I guess people generally think of Portland as bland.

Portland is lovely.

Except for the snakes. When I was very young, one found its way into our backyard, and as I knelt to examine it, my mother ran outside from the kitchen and killed it with a shovel.

My mother was very beautiful—poised and stylish too. I don't want you to get a Wild-Wild-West kind of impression of her. It's just that desperate women do desperate things.

That I can assure you.

My father was an architect. Fifteen years after the snake incident, he taught me how to parallel-park in that way people do when they are engineers in their souls and understand physics in their brains, and are teaching people who are writers in their souls and understand poetry in their brains. We laugh about it now.

I spent every summer of my youth on Cape Cod, aboard a little boat, hauling in blues and bass by the cooler-full. For the record, and with God as my witness, I felt for the fish.

I went to college, became a journalist in Miami, watched the city burn twice, moved North, landed a job at the Associated Press, got married, went to business school, became a management consultant, and worked very hard to look like I knew something meaningful about industrial manufacturing.

I was later the editor of the *Harvard Business Review,* until I was fired.

At the age of forty-one, I got divorced. It was the right thing to do.

Three years later, I got married again. It was the rightest thing I've ever done.

I have four children. Actually, they're not really children anymore. But they're my children.

Not a one of them looks like me. Two are fair Nordic types; they look like Swedish farmhands. But even the two dark ones look like strangers by my side. It's OK—truly. It's a good reminder that they should have their own lives.

If I had a magic wand, though, I'd use it to teach my kids everything I know with a little tap on the forehead. Because like most parents, I wish they could skip all the hard parts.

They won't. And I guess that's OK too. As the Russian novelist Fyodor Dostoevsky once observed, "Suffering is the sole origin of consciousness." Learning how to live from experience is part of the human condition.

Still, there is just one thing I wish I could teach my kids without all the blood, sweat, and tears usually involved.

10-10-10

How to make good decisions.

Simply put, that is what this book is about—a new approach to making choices that will allow you to create a life of your own making, no matter where you were born, how you've spent your days, and what mistakes you've made along the way.

It's about a steady discipline that can help us replace chaos with consistency, confusion with clarity, and perhaps best of all, guilt with not-guilt, or to use another word for that condition, joy.

It's about an idea that changed my life and has transformed the lives of men and women around the world.

Now—please! I'm not suggesting that I've got it all tied up in a bow. There are still plenty of times when I can't get out of my own way with my bright ideas and best-laid plans. And I know, too, that sometimes life is formed by chance or by events outside our control. Accidents and miracles happen. Of course they do.

But much more often, our lives are formed by decisions within our control, though it may not feel that way. In today's accelerated world, with its streaming information, confounding options, uncertain global economy, and ever-morphing culture, many of the decisions we face can seem unspeakably complicated, or as if there are just too many of them, in too little time. So we decide by not deciding or by letting our gut instinct guide us. We ask our friends for advice, consulting them like Ouija boards, or we look for signs, the way ancient people sought counsel in oracle bones. And we hope for the best.

Today, my life is renewed; my decisions deliberate,

purposeful, and confident. But thirteen years ago, I was there, in that hoping place. Even with my credentials and accomplishments, my loving family, and dear friends, even with the affection and respect I was blessed to receive, I made many of my decisions as if I was watching them from a moving car. Sometimes things worked out. More often, they didn't. And my life showed it. It was fine one day or week or month, then crazy. It was tedious, then frustrating, then all wrong, then all right. It was happy and full, then lonely. It was moving forward, it was falling back.

I wasn't living my life. My life was living me.

Then came February 1996. I was in Hawaii, though not for a vacation. With a full-time job at the *Harvard Business Review,* four children under the age of six, and a rocky marriage, I didn't take a lot of vacations in those days. I was in Hawaii to deliver a speech to a convention of insurance executives who had offered to pay me a mortgage coupon's worth of dollars to enlighten them about the history of management.

My boss was thrilled about my trip. I was, as she put it, "getting the brand out there." But I knew that I couldn't leave my husband alone in charge of four kids. So I decided I could make it work for everyone if I brought my five- and six-year-olds along. Not to worry, I assured the trip's organizer. The clients might be "extremely demanding"—her words exactly—but my kids were extremely mature. They were practically little adults! "The clients won't even notice they're there," I promised.

Back home, I gathered Roscoe and Sophia into my arms. "We're going on a wonderful adventure," I told them. "Mommy has to work a little with some clients. But you won't even notice they're there!"

With one clever plan, I had finally cracked the work-life balance code, all while putting money in the bank! Or so I had "decided." Hooray for me.

Hooray, it turned out, for the saintly flight attendant on our plane. Because she did not kill me when Sophia spent the entire twelve-hour flight demonstrating the use of those little white air-sickness bags. My poor lovely thing. She was green by the time we landed. Not to worry, though, I thought—a few hours at the beach will do her a world of good. It will do wonders for all of us. Family time! Sand castles, body surfing, happy memories!

And sun poisoning. No, I didn't forget sunscreen. I over-remembered it, slathering ladlefuls on Roscoe's luminous Nordic skin and then covering him with a shirt, hat, and towel for good measure. Prudent mother that I was, I had turned my little boy into a convection oven.

Not surprisingly, what with the ice packs and soothing I needed to apply to stop the wailing, I ended up arriving late to the client's festivities that evening. To compensate, however, I immediately leaped into mingle-and-chat mode, introducing myself to everyone.

My approach seemed to be working well enough—these were insurance executives after a day on the golf course—but I did notice a group of people at the party who didn't really seem inclined to mingle and chat back with me. It wasn't the attendees themselves, but their wives. Perhaps they were wondering where my husband was. Or maybe they thought, correctly, that I looked as frantic as a woman who had two moaning kids up in her room and a speech to give the next morning.

Hours later, the party ended and I rushed back to the kids, staying up with them most of the night, as all three of us battled jet lag—then each other. They wanted *The Little Mermaid,* I wanted the headline news. They wanted one more story about Nonnie and the snake. I wanted to close my eyes.

At 5 AM, to win the peace, I ordered ice cream for breakfast and, finally, sticky faces pressed close, we slept.

Not for long, though. At nine, I sent the kids off to a hotel-run hula dancing camp on the beach and dutifully donned my power suit. Then I climbed the stairs to center stage, and pointer in hand, spent the next hour marching my bleary-eyed audience through Frederick Taylor's four principles of scientific management, Max Weber's seminal insights into command-and-control hierarchies, and Peter Drucker's groundbreaking views on outsourcing. I may not have been exactly scintillating, but I was earning my keep, one PowerPoint slide at a time.

Until, that is, the very last moments of my speech when, gazing toward the back of the auditorium, I noticed that two little people were trying to get into the room, their bodies pressed against the sliding glass doors, hands cupped around their eyes to peer in all the more intently.

It was Roscoe and Sophia, dressed in hula skirts. They'd made a jail break and come to hunt me down.

Up on stage, I wrapped things up with a quick thud—no Q & A as planned—then bolted toward the back of the room to head them off. I'll never forget how they frantically grabbed my legs when I reached them, or how the insurance executives who caught the scene regarded me, eyebrows raised high.

Yes, yes, I realize now that I should have packed my bags at that point and headed home. But in my make-everyone-happy, I-can-freaking-do-it-all mind, I still had twenty-four hours to go. I promptly decided I would spend the rest of the day scuba diving with the kids, tire them out, put them to bed, then show up at the client's luau ready to charm until sunrise if need be.

I didn't count on the saltwater making Roscoe shriek or the luau actually lasting until nearly sunrise, by which time I was decidedly not charming. I was confused and exhausted to the point of weepiness. At one point, I even put my head down on a table and shut my eyes. When I opened them again, I saw a client-wife looking down at me with a mordant grin. "You working mothers," she said, voice dripping with vinegar, "I don't know how you do it all."

"Just smoke and mirrors," I blithered.

"Your husband must be very patient," she responded archly.

"Oh, he most certainly is," I assured her.

With that big piñata of a lie hanging between us, the client-wife wandered off. Eventually, I wandered off too, to my room, bedraggled. I sent the babysitter away and collapsed into a chair on the balcony. A glorious, big golden sun—just like in the postcards—was lifting toward the creamy blue sky of morning above.

I didn't know it at the time, but a new day was indeed breaking.

"I have to end this craziness," I heard myself saying. I might have fallen asleep for a moment there, or I might have just zoned out. My consciousness was fading in and out like a cell phone call from a mountain pass. "I have to figure out another way," I muttered.

I don't know what happened next, or why, and I probably never will.

Perhaps I had simply reached the point where change had to happen; no alternative remained. Or maybe that trip was the last factor in the equation of experiences that added up to some nascent form of judgment, or vision, or understanding. Maybe I simply received a gift. All I know for sure is that, as the sun rose over the sea, an idea came into my mind.

It was a lifeline and my lifesaver from that moment forward.

It was the beginning of a journey of discovery and reinvention that I took myself, and that we are about to take together.

It was 10-10-10.

CHAPTER ONE

It Was What?

10-10-10 in the Light of Day

To tell you the truth, I didn't know precisely what 10-10-10 was at the moment of its inception, except that I suddenly felt as if I had a new, different, and massively better operating principle in my (albeit tenuous) grasp. I had come upon, it seemed, an enhanced thinking process of sorts, a methodology for getting systematic about things. All I *really* had to do to reclaim my life, I realized that morning on my Hawaiian balcony, was to start making my decisions differently—proactively—by deliberately considering their consequences in the immediate present, near term, and distant future.

In ten minutes . . . ten months . . . and ten years.

If I did that, I figured with a fair amount of wonder, I might actually have my very own "life management tool."

And thirteen years later, that term continues to be how I define 10-10-10 in quick and easy shorthand. That said, I've certainly heard 10-10-10 described in other ways. One dedicated 10-10-10 practitioner I know calls it "a road map for clarity and courage," another, "my little guilt eraser." A grandmother from Houston once told me she refers to 10-10-10 as her "kick-start to get unfrozen." A Canadian minister who has preached about 10-10-10 describes it as "a great bridge enabling us to put things in perspective."

But none of those handles for 10-10-10—mine included—really describe the nitty-gritty logistics of the process. So before we go any further, let's break them down.

THE HOW OF 10-10-10

Every 10-10-10 process starts with a question. That is, every 10-10-10 begins with posing your dilemma, crisis, or problem in the form of a query. Should I quit my job? Should I buy the house with the great backyard and leaky roof? Should I hold my son back a year in school? Should I stay in my relationship or end it?

Having a defined question is essential to 10-10-10, I've come to discover, because so many messy problems are intertwined with side issues and sub-issues, distractions and digressions, red herrings and bit players. Thus, the most effective 10-10-10s always tend to start with determining exactly what issue, underneath it all, you're trying to resolve.

The next stage of 10-10-10 is data collection. Not to worry; you can conduct this part of the process in your head, on your computer, with pen and paper, or in conversation with a friend or partner—whatever works. The only real "requirement" is that you be honest and exhaustive in answering the following prompts:

Given my question, what are the consequences of each of my options in ten minutes?

In ten months?

In ten years?

Now, to be clear, there is nothing *literal* about each ten in 10-10-10. The first 10 basically stands for "right now"—as in, one minute, one hour, or one week. The second 10 represents that point in the foreseeable future when the initial reaction to your decision has passed but its consequences continue to play out in ways you can reasonably predict. And the third 10 stands for a time in a future that is so far off that its particulars are entirely vague. So, really, 10-10-10 could just as well be referring to nine days, fifteen months, and twenty years, or two hours, six months, and eight years. The name of the process is just a totem meant to directionally suggest time frames along the lines of: in the heat of the moment, somewhat later, and when all is said and done.

The last step of the 10-10-10 process is analysis. For this stage, you need to take all the information you've just compiled and compare it to your innermost values—your beliefs, goals, dreams, and needs. In short, this part of 10-10-10 impels you to ask: "Knowing what I now know about all of my options and their consequences, which decision will best help me create a life of my own making?"

And with the answer to that, you have your 10-10-10 solution.

IN THE BEGINNING

As I've said, a fully conceptualized version of 10-10-10, logistics and all, didn't exactly strike me like a thunderbolt that Hawaiian morning. Rather, my thinking was more like, "I have to stop running around tamping down fires and trying to make everyone happy. When the kids are in their twenties, they're going to love me or hate me for decisions far bigger than whether or not I took them on a four-day business trip in February 1996. I'm just living too much in the moment, for God's sake."

And with that, I formed the concept of "10-10." I was going to start making my decisions based on a balance of short-term and long-term considerations. What nonsense it had been, I told myself, to have schlepped the kids five thousand miles for a few piddling swims on the beach together. If I had left them home, their pouting would have lasted a day at most, had there even been any.

Almost instantly, however, I became aware of the incompleteness of my emergent idea. Over the next few months, I was actually going to be away from home twice more, for a wedding and then for another conference. Maybe my trip to Hawaii, taken cumulatively, had me absent from the children too much. Maybe, for true balance and perspective, my new decision-making process needed to consider a more middle-term horizon as well.

Thus 10-10-10 was officially born.

With nothing to lose, I started applying the process to all sorts of dilemmas both at home and work as soon as we returned to Boston. Should I stay at the office for an emergency when I promised the kids I'd be home at six? Should I spend the holidays with my parents or my in-laws? Should I confront a difficult writer about a late manuscript? Should I focus my time on an article submitted by a promising newcomer or a steady old-timer? Much to my surprise, I found that the process *invariably* led me to faster, cleaner, and sounder decisions. And as an unexpected bonus, it also gave me a way to explain myself to all the relevant "constituents"—my kids or parents or boss—with clarity and confidence. "Let me tell you how I came to that decision," I could finally say, and go from there.

Within months, 10-10-10 had served me so well that I couldn't resist sharing it with my sisters, Elin and Della, as well as a cadre of close friends and colleagues.

And so it was that the process first started to spread. One of my coworkers told his wife, who used it to untangle herself from a state of job-search paralysis. A friend "gave" 10-10-10 to her just-married daughter, who was struggling with whether to continue working or return to graduate school. Another acquaintance of mine described 10-10-10 to her husband, a doctor, and he brought it to work, where a group of nurses adopted it to confront—and resolve—a contentious dispute over patient visiting hours that had been simmering for months.

Eventually, 10-10-10 stories from outside my immediate circle began to trickle back to me. One day, for instance, I answered my phone to hear, "Are you the 10-10-10 lady?"

When I figured out that I was and said as much, my caller burst into friendly laughter and identified herself as

Gwen, the sister of one of the nurses. "Sorry to surprise you," she said, "but I'm calling because I'm sitting here wishing you could see me. I'm smiling for the first time in months."

Gwen, it turned out, was a stay-at-home mother in Chicago. Like her sister, she had started with a career in nursing, but she had changed course after a few years to become a sales rep for a pharmaceutical company. The job was a perfect fit for Gwen's outgoing personality and professional drive. "You couldn't peel me away from my sales rounds," she told me. "It wasn't work to me. It was fun. Oh—and the money! It couldn't have been better."

Gwen enjoyed her career so thoroughly that she barely missed a beat through the pregnancies and births of her three children. Sure, there were challenging times when her job and motherhood collided, but she always felt supported by her husband, who was also a sales rep, in her choice to keep working. The couple hired a live-in nanny and communicated with her constantly by cell phone. They spent weekends reconnecting with each other and their kids.

One evening when Gwen returned from yet another long stretch on the road, however, her nanny put her fifteen-month-old son in her arms and he didn't recognize her, shoving her away with an angry squeal. Gwen was shaken to her core. Her husband, looking on, was too.

Overwhelmed by a growing sense of guilt, Gwen soon resigned. "I'll be back in a few months," she promised her boss, "just as soon as things get back to normal at home."

But weeks passed, then months, and bit by bit, Gwen found herself ever more entrenched in the "back to normal" she was trying to build, her days busy with driving the kids to lessons, friends' houses, and various and sundry appointments, her nights taken over by dinner, homework, baths, and story time. Her office off the family's garage, piled with the industry trade magazines she vowed to keep reading, began to fill up with skate sharpeners and costumes for the school play.

After a year at home, Gwen's heart started to fill too—not with sadness, but with a vague, persistent longing for the big career that could have been. Occasionally, she would reread an email from her old boss she couldn't bring herself to delete from her inbox. "We'll take you back whenever you want," it said. "Your old team needs you and misses you."

Gwen missed them too, but how much? Weeks passed with her mind seesawing in debate. Had she really chosen stay-at-home motherhood, she wondered, or had she fallen into it by not choosing otherwise?

In the middle of this quandary, Gwen's sister mentioned 10-10-10 to her, suggesting she might use it the next time she felt stuck.

That happened a few days later. "I was cleaning the refrigerator, my hands and face covered with cold water and detergent, everything melting all over the place, and Sammy was crying his head off. I just lost it," Gwen told me. "For once and for all, I needed to decide if I should keep being a full-time mom."

Gwen soothed Sammy and put him down for a nap,

finished with the refrigerator, and poured herself a cup of coffee. Then, with an hour to spare before her daughter arrived home from school, she sat in her kitchen and started to 10-10-10.

Her very first emotion, as the process unfolded, was dread. "Short term, if I stayed home, I knew I was looking at a lot of diapers and spit-up, with my brain not really in high gear," she told me. "I was looking at a bit of boredom, and a lot of wondering about what might have been." As for the long-term, ten-year scenario, "I knew the kids would basically be on their way out the door by that time," Gwen said. "They would be gone, and so would my career."

But a different kind of revelation began to emerge as Gwen considered the ten-month scenario. "Suddenly, as I sat there thinking about it, I became conscious of how much I cared about the time in between the first and last 10s," she said. "When Sammy makes his first goal, Emma has her first flute recital, and Alex learns to shave, I'll be there. I realized I was giving up one dream, but I was getting a reality I couldn't walk away from in return."

Another mother might have landed at a different conclusion that day in the kitchen, but for Gwen, 10-10-10 crystallized her priorities. Her decision didn't mean she would jump for joy every time the baby cried; it didn't mean that she would delight in the hours spent waiting for ice hockey practice to end. It simply meant she had made a values-driven choice that she could—and wanted to—live by.

THE TOUGH STUFF

No wonder Gwen was smiling when she first tracked me down. Her ambivalence was gone—and in its place, the peace of mind that comes with intentionality. But for the sake of full disclosure, you need to know right here and now that every 10-10-10 process doesn't end so neatly. Sometimes the solution you arrive at will be an outright surprise, as the process can surface values, agendas, fears, and dreams you've never confronted before, or it can send you down paths you've long avoided in order to keep your world under control. Some 10-10-10 solutions can even be deeply challenging, as they "require" you to come clean with others about what you truly believe and how you want to live. The truth is, transformation doesn't always come easily.

About a year ago, I gave a speech about 10-10-10 on a college campus. Afterward, one student lingered, waiting to see me alone.

He was, it turned out, an aspiring entrepreneur from Romania named Razvan, who wanted to launch a mobile phone company back home. The problem, he quickly told me, was that his longtime girlfriend, a waitress waiting for him in Bucharest, wanted to launch it with him. "What happens when Mihaela makes a mistake with a contract or something? She's not very tough when it comes to money; her family was all Communist," he reported matter-of-factly. "Then I have to say, 'Mihaela, we're trying to make a profit here,' and she starts yelling, 'Profit, forget profit—

what about ideals?' And we have a fight, like always. You know what I mean?"

I got the picture, at least enough to get started. I gestured for Razvan to step closer, so we could conduct a 10-10-10 together about whether he should work with Mihaela on his new business venture.

In ten minutes, a "yes" answer was enormously appealing, Razvan said eagerly. Mihaela would calm down and, at least for a while, throw her best energies into the project. A "no" answer would cause, in Razvan's words, "World War Three," as Mihaela's family and his own—they were close friends—were sure to get involved and lobby him to change his mind.

The ten-month picture was less mixed; it would be grim no matter which choice was made. If they worked together, Razvan said, he and Mihaela would likely be back to their quarreling. But apart, there would be misery too: "We've been together for many years and there is love between us," he reflected wistfully.

We turned to the ten-year picture, and right away Razvan grimaced as if he was seeing a photograph that disturbed him. If he asked Mihaela to join his venture, they would surely be married by then, an outcome guaranteeing, as he put it, "a life of daily battles."

"Because your hopes and dreams are fundamentally different?" I asked.

"Because all we really have is history," he replied. "And I know that's not enough. We will spend our lives hurting each other."

With that, Razvan's 10-10-10 decision was made.

Was he happy? Of course not. Indeed, as we parted, I could see tears welling in his eyes. But I could also tell he was relieved in some measure, and resolved too, about taking control of his life and his future. Happiness, he seemed to know, awaited him. Sometimes, that is all 10-10-10 can promise.

A TRICKLE TO A WAVE

By 2006, I had heard enough stories from people like Gwen and Razvan to get the feeling that I was on to something with 10-10-10. And so I decided to write about the process in *O, The Oprah Magazine,* where I have a regular column about work-life balance.

My "on to something" feeling, however, did not prepare me for the response. Heartfelt emails and letters soon poured in. 10-10-10, I discovered, wasn't just useful within one or two or three degrees of separation. It worked for men and women, young and old, near and far, in decisions large and small and in-between, at home and at work, and in love, friendship, and parenting.

It even worked for a twenty-seven-year-old government employee named Antoine Jefferson, who wrote me to say that he was using 10-10-10 to guide him in his personal goal of reinventing the welfare system, one act of kindness at a time.

What the heck, I wondered, is this guy talking about?

And so I called Antoine, and later had the great pleasure of meeting him in his native city of Philadelphia, where hearing his story convinced me that 10-10-10 can work effectively in ways and places I had never imagined.

Raised by a single mother in a neighborhood of housing projects, Antoine stopped going to school in seventh grade, and was eventually moved into foster care, where he was bounced among five different families. His days were often lonely, filled mainly with television-watching alone; he missed his siblings painfully. But perhaps the most defining experience of Antoine's life was the realization, at age thirteen or fourteen, that he wasn't like anyone he knew. Not just because he was gay, but because he was so unrelentingly optimistic. Even with all its harshness, the world could be a better place, Antoine believed, if people just stopped hurting each other.

A few months before my article was published, Antoine was hired to work at one of the state's busiest welfare offices, greeting clients and directing them through the application process. The idea of helping people in need thrilled him at first. But his excitement soon turned to despair. All around him every day, he saw his coworkers address the people coming into the office rudely and dismissively. "Applying for welfare usually happens at your lowest moment in life. There is so much shame in it," he told me. "The system is supposed to be about lifting people up, not breaking them more."

One night after work, Antoine wrote an impassioned manifesto about the ways he thought office protocol should change. They were fighting words, he knew, and when he showed them to his sister Tiffany, she gently tried to warn him off. "Everyone is going to hate you, Antoine," she said.

For the next few hours, Antoine sorted through the 10-10-10 consequences of presenting his proposal at work.

In ten minutes, he reasoned, there would be hell to pay. He had expressed his views to his coworkers already, and they'd brushed him off. Their message, as he heard it, was "Stop rocking the boat."

In ten months, Antoine predicted, the contentiousness with his colleagues would surely remain, or even worsen, as he refused to back down from his role as the office cop. On the other hand, if Antoine stayed mum, he worried that a crushing sense of hypocrisy would likely be destroying him inside. Neither option appealed.

But Antoine's path of action became clear as soon as he considered the ten-year scenario. "I realized I was absolutely willing to take the heat—and I even *wanted* to take it—for the chance to improve the welfare system of this state," he said. "All I could think was, 'If not me, who?' Someone has to lead change, even on the lowest rungs of the ladder."

The next day, Antoine met with his boss to describe his concerns about the cynicism that pervaded the office and the mistreatment of its patrons. She received his manifesto very positively, he recalls. But after she brought it to a meeting with the whole staff, Antoine's coworkers, as expected, started to freeze him out.

Rather than manage the mess, Antoine's boss asked him if he would be willing to be transferred to another welfare office across town.

He agreed. "I wasn't sorry or angry for a second," he told me recently. "I feel as if I did the right thing."

Today, Antoine continues to 10-10-10 any and all dilemmas that he encounters both at home and work. In fact, he recently shared the process with his mother, who, he says, immediately used it to make what could prove to be a transformative decision of her own. At the age of fifty-four, she's entered a training program in hopes of starting a small business someday. "I believe this is the beginning of a whole new life for my mother," Antoine says. "For the first time, I see her trying to create her own future."

ABOUT THAT THIRD 10

How exciting that new journey sounds. 10-10-10 does have a way of galvanizing people into forward-thinking action and out of a fixation on the present. But it would be a mistake to think that the *only* purpose of 10-10-10 is to clang long-term alarm bells during the decision-making process.

Yes, heightening your awareness of ten years out is one purpose of 10-10-10, and a very good one. All too often, we make decisions just to avoid an immediate ouch—the sulking child, the disappointed family, the complicated logistics, the angry coworkers, and so on. The third 10 in 10-10-10 has a powerful way of mitigating that tendency. It helps us decide whether (or not) it's worth it to endure short-term flame-outs in the service of our larger, more deeply held goals in life.

No one, however, should make *every* decision based on its consequences in the long term. First, such prudence is pretty much guaranteed to make your day-to-day life a total bore. You cannot banish spontaneity! But the main reason not to set your sights exclusively on the third 10 is that it can be too damn risky.

Pete Turkel taught me that.

Pete was an editor on the swing shift at the Associated Press back in the mid-1980s, when I was all of twenty-six years old and a reporter in the Boston bureau. At the time I met Pete, I was working the overnight shift myself, reporting for duty at midnight and released to freedom at 8 AM when, oddly enough, I found myself hungry for a burger and a beer. My skewed body clock was unpleasant enough, but at least I was still able to see friends and family at breakfast and dinner. Pete, who came in at 4 PM and left at midnight, missed *everything*. He was asleep when his kids left for school and his wife for work, and he was at work when they all came home, ate dinner, and went to bed.

One day, bitching and moaning about my own hours, I turned to Pete—twenty years my senior—and blurted out, "I don't know how *you* stand it. It's like you're living on another planet or something."

To this day, I admire Pete for not smacking me for my temerity. Instead he smiled in his familiar, good-hearted way. "You'll understand this when you're older, Suzy, and have real bills to pay and a family to raise," he said. "I'm paid a premium for working this shift. If I keep at this job, I'll be able to retire early, send my kids to college without loans, and buy a house with a dock on a lake. What I'm doing will be worth every minute of it when I walk out that door on my last day."

I was one year gone from the AP when Pete was killed in a car crash. (His wife was gravely injured and died later.) But it was never lost on me that Pete was postponing life—for all the "right" reasons—at the time of his death.

I still think about Pete. His life reminds me that while it's important to consider the long-term consequences of every 10-10-10 decision, they cannot be *consistently* more important than the short- and midterm. The far-off future often matters more than we give it credit for and should influence our thinking more than it usually does. But it should not trump all other time frame considerations, all the time.

TURNAROUND TIME

If there is one piece of push back I receive about 10-10-10, it concerns timing and it generally goes like this: "I'm just too busy to do that kind of thing."

With life-changing decisions, it's true that 10-10-10 can take hours or longer to conduct. Later on, we will meet an advertising executive who leaned on 10-10-10 to help her decide what to do about her career after her son was diagnosed with a genetic mental illness. Because it required the gathering of medical opinions, her 10-10-10 decision unfurled over the course of two weeks.

Far more often, however, 10-10-10 slows you down

just enough to get your decision right. It doesn't squander your time as much as invests it wisely.

Take Natalie, a tech company manager I met last year. Along with her busy job, Natalie tries to stay deeply present in the lives of her two teenage sons, both high school athletes, and her husband of eighteen years. Most days, she keeps all of her balls in the air, but when a new one gets tossed into the mix, sometimes unexpected decisions need to be made—quickly.

Natalie's uncle, Charlie, had never been a big part of her life, but when he passed away at the age of eighty-three, Natalie felt more conflicted than she had expected about attending his funeral service. "I barely knew him. He was my mother's brother-in-law," she explained to me. "But I also knew that showing up would mean the world to my parents and the rest of my extended family. They would take it as a sign of respect."

With that realization, Natalie decided she needed to be at the ceremony. She made plans to leave work early, but just as she was about to head out the door, her fifteen-year-old son text-messaged her. His lift to soccer practice had fallen through; could she help? Before Natalie could even react, another text message came in, this one from her husband. He had to stay late at work. Could she cover for him and drive their younger son to the orthodontist?

"Well, there goes the funeral," Natalie groaned in frustration, picking up the phone to call her mother.

But then she stopped. Why not, she reasoned, 10-10-10 the problem? She had learned about the process from another working mother, and had been using it ever since to sort out the kind of mini work-life balance conflicts that come with the territory.

With that, she quickly defined her immediate question as, "Should I attend Uncle Charlie's funeral?"

In ten minutes, she knew a "no" would make her life flat-out easier. She wouldn't have to find another ride for Josh, or go through the elaborate dance of rescheduling Todd's appointment with the recalcitrant receptionist at the orthodontist's office. What a relief.

In ten months though, the consequence of a no-go decision made Natalie cringe. She only had one chance to bid her uncle goodbye. More than that, she probably wouldn't have another opportunity to see several of her elderly relatives who were quite dear to her.

And what about the consequences in ten years? As a parent, Natalie was a firm believer in the old saw, "Actions speak louder than words." If she wanted to teach her children the values of respect and responsibility, she had to demonstrate them herself.

The next number she dialed was her son's cell phone. "Josh, I can't help you," she told her older boy. "It's very important for me to attend my uncle's funeral—to show my family how much I love them. Please ask Coach to help you find a lift." She then called her son's orthodontist and canceled his appointment; she'd reschedule it, she figured, when she found the time.

Finally, on the road to her family's church, she called her husband to explain her choice. "I'm with you," he said when she was done. At first, Natalie thought he was simply saying, "I'm on your side." Instead, he meant it literally.

He dropped an email to his boss and jumped in his own car—to be with Natalie at the service.

Later, when I asked Natalie how much time she spent on her 10-10-10 decision, she laughed in surprise. "Oh, I don't know," she said, "maybe two minutes."

But I wasn't surprised. I've seen 10-10-10 sort out even longer-brewing dilemmas just as quickly.

One summer evening a few years ago, I was chopping onions for dinner when my daughter Sophia wandered by the kitchen. The hula-dancing incident long behind her, she had grown into a young woman who loved to write, mimicked me to perfection, and could hit a wicked two-handed backhand. She had the varsity letters framed in her bedroom to prove it.

"Mom, I need to tell you something," she said quietly. "I'm quitting tennis."

My heart sank. Over the previous year, I'd certainly noticed Sophia cutting her practices short and, when I let myself listen, I'd certainly heard her complaining that she wasn't finding joy in the game anymore. But that had never kept me from hoping she was in a phase that would pass.

I stopped what I was doing and put on the steadiest voice I could muster.

"Absolutely, positively, one hundred percent *no,*" I said. "We've worked too hard and spent too many hours to get where we are to give it all up now."

I expected a fight, but Sophia surprised me. Perfectly calm, she shrugged and simply replied, "OK, but let's 10-10-10 it. How about framing up the question as: '*Should Sophia stop playing a game that she's sick of?*'"

"I would prefer it without the editorializing," I said, "but fine."

Sophia started by stating her case. In all three time frames, she said, freedom from tennis would allow her to focus on interests she simply and truly enjoyed more. And she insisted that she wouldn't stop playing tennis entirely, she would keep at it, only recreationally.

"Colleges want varsity letters," I resisted, "and in about ten months, that's going to matter. Colleges want kids who stick with things, who don't give up when things get hard."

"Colleges should see the real Sophia," came the answer, "and I'm not playing tennis in college, Mom. Come on, I'm not good enough. It's not fun for me to keep getting beaten. It's not my sport. It's yours."

She was right, of course, but I wasn't ready to surrender.

"When you're a grown-up, ten, twenty years from now, you're going to wish you could play tennis with friends," I said. "And with me. We could play together."

"I could destroy you and your pathetic serve with one hand tied behind my back," Sophia said with the beginnings of a smile. She waited a moment before her final shot; I suppose she knew it was a winner. "Mom," she said, "this decision is about *my* life."

With that I had to smile too. The game was over, and Sophia had won it fair and square. 10-10-10 had been there as our trusted referee.

SEEING WHAT WE NEED TO

And 10-10-10 is always there. No matter what the scope of the dilemma it's applied to, no matter what the details. Since the morning that I found 10-10-10, or it found me, I have seen the idea evolve into its full form and spread from person to person, across boundaries of every kind.

Because it works.

In a time when the world moves at warp speed and decisions can feel inexorably complex, 10-10-10 can help you forge an intentional life, choice by choice. It can make you far less likely to find yourself outside looking in at your life, in shock, dismay, or the kind of regret that rusts in you forever. It helps you decide whether you want to be a career woman or a mother, or both, whether a relationship should go forward or end, or if a job is worth saving.

10-10-10 adds reason where it is lacking. It inserts deliberation where there is only instinct. It replaces opaqueness with transparency.

Or as Antoine told me once, 10-10-10 "hushes the noise so the mind can see what it needs to."

Which brings me back to my first description of 10-10-10 as a life-management tool.

The truth is, if you use 10-10-10 consistently, it becomes less of a tool or a process or a device or a methodology—and more of an infinite and sustaining heartbeat.

It becomes a way of life.

CHAPTER TWO

This Is Your Brain on 10-10-10

The Science Behind the System

One day when I was talking with Antoine Jefferson about his change campaign at the welfare department, it dawned on me to ask him how he had made decisions before he found 10-10-10. The question produced a long sigh. "Well, just gut, I suppose," he said, shaking his head as if the memory both amused and mystified him. "And let me tell you, when I made all my decisions by the seat of my pants, I was on my ass *a lot*."

I heard similar admissions from virtually every person I interviewed for this book. "For thirty years, I let my stomach guide me," a schoolteacher in California told me. "I called it my 'uh-oh' feeling, and it worked about thirty percent of the time." A mother of three in New Jersey said that she had asked her husband and friends for advice and then picked the point of view she liked the most. "No one ever knew where I was coming from," she recalled.

Another 10-10-10er confessed, "I suppose I just waited for decisions to happen to me."

These kinds of comments got me wondering: If 10-10-10 was so successful in changing the way people approached decision making, how were decisions *usually* made? And how did 10-10-10 help people make them differently?

A BEAUTIFUL MIND

Now, I'm no scientist. The last time I was in a laboratory, I was dissecting a fetal pig that my classmate and I had dubbed Johnny Rotten. But for the past two years, I've been on a small mission to learn about how the brain works, guided by willing experts in psychology, neurology, behavioral economics, and evolutionary biology. Their insights, along with those limned from a pile of scientific texts, have unlocked some of my own about how and why 10-10-10 works so effectively.

The human mind, I've come to learn, is a wondrous product of evolution, designed to guide and protect us in the most common social situations. We excel, for example, at forming alliances, making deals, and discerning motives. We're good at picking leaders, working in teams, and sensing enemies posing as friends. Such skills came in very handy as human beings struggled to survive in the earliest days of civilization, and thanks to the process of natural selection, they carry on in our neurological "wiring" today.

While we can handle many types of social interactions

with highly evolved aptitude, however, our minds are not nearly as adept at making decisions with multiple variables and time frames—and for good reason. As a species, human beings tend to place a decreasing value on both gains and losses as they stretch into the future. The psychological lingo for this dynamic is "hyperbolic discounting," which, in everyday parlance, essentially means that people tend to act as if the future doesn't exist or that it will be ideal.

There are countless studies that demonstrate this effect. A 1999 report published by the Johns Hopkins School of Medicine, for instance, found that as many as 80 percent of the people who undergo an excruciating coronary bypass do not make the relatively easy lifestyle changes required to prevent further surgery, continuing to eat fatty foods, smoke cigarettes, and avoid the treadmill.

But scientific research is hardly necessary to confirm that we routinely ignore the long-term impact of our actions. We've all said yes to an invitation to go somewhere or a request to help someone, knowing full well that we will be too busy to fulfill the commitment when the time comes. We've all skipped exercise, downed another glass of wine, or finished off the last of the brownies. Somewhere in our visceral psyches, at least to some extent, we've all bought into the age-old "Eat, drink, and be merry, for tomorrow we all may die" mind-set.

Few people, of course, operate *solely* in the present tense. Clearly, it's also within our nature to develop coping mechanisms to combat hyperbolic discounting and "force" long-term considerations into our decision-making process.

Some people keep journals to hear themselves think; others compile scrupulous lists of pros and cons. I have some friends who never make a decision without praying about it, and others who live by the credo "Never decide alone." Before 10-10-10 entered my life, collective pondering was my favored approach too, when I had one. I'd try to run my messiest dilemmas by my sisters, both of whom were very good at asking down-the-road-type questions.

But let's be real. Few decisions occur in situations where we can turn to a journal or even a pair of level-headed sisters for the kind of 360-degree perspective we need. At the end of the day, many of our choices are so personal and so complicated that, by necessity and convention, we are alone with them.

And that's where 10-10-10 comes in. By bringing every option and its consequences to the surface and connecting actions to deeply held values, the process empowers us to override the counterproductive tendencies of our own minds. It helps us help ourselves.

GREAT EXPECTATIONS

To understand how 10-10-10 achieves that effect, we need to go back (very briefly!) to the eighteenth century. In 1738, a Dutch-Swiss mathematician named Daniel Bernoulli postulated that people facing decisions with multiple variables would survey the likelihood and severity of possible outcomes and assess the consequences of each, then choose the option that would maximize their gains and minimize their losses across all time frames. Or in essence, they would try to get the most personal "value," or upside, out of any decision.

Bernoulli's idea was so intriguing that two centuries later it was embraced and more fully developed by two renowned mathematicians from Princeton University, John von Neumann and Oskar Morgenstern, who termed it "Expected Utility Theory."

The problem with Expected Utility Theory, though, is that it has a rather inconsistent relationship with reality. People do not regularly survey the likelihood and severity of all of their choices. They do not habitually assess outcomes and consequences. They do not, in other words, act rationally all of the time.

The forces that undermine rationality in human behavior are many, most of them quite familiar to anyone who's, well, alive. There's time pressure, peer pressure, lack of information, and information overload. The list goes on. But the result of all these conditions is stress, the ultimate deterrent to rational thinking. When it kicks in, our blood pressure rises, our pulse quickens, and adrenaline rushes through our veins. Sometimes these reactions can be all for the good, sharpening our focus and intent, allowing us to act almost superhuman. My friend Skye, for instance, jumped out of the driver's seat after a terrible car crash and rescued her sister, who was strapped in the back. Not until later, when her sister was safe and sound, did Skye notice that she was hurt. She had a shattered pelvis.

But outside of such do-or-die emergencies, stress much more typically interferes with sound decision making. As stress hormones race throughout the body, they monopolize the prefrontal cortex, an area of the brain where complex reasoning occurs. And when stress ramps up into full-blown anxiety, our misfiring neurotransmitters can provoke what some psychologists call "closed-loop thinking," in which the mind starts to fixate on a single worry, like a song you can't get out of your head. The result can be feelings of confusion or paralysis—or both. I suspect that just before my 10-10-10 epiphany in Hawaii, my own poor brain, clamoring with the voices of people who had a stake in my life choices, was experiencing exactly such a meltdown.

I was rescued by the sunrise and an idea.

Most people, however, are rescued from stressful indecision by their brain's back-up generator: gut instinct.

SUBCONSCIOUSLY SPEAKING

Not long ago, while I was getting rehabilitation for a bum elbow, my physical therapist asked me what my ailing joint had been "telling" me lately. "You have to listen to your body," she said. "It's like your gut—filled with wisdom."

I nodded; like most everyone, I would agree that gut instinct has its moments of blazing insight. It's a pattern recognizer, if you will. It's your subconscious saying, "Hello, you've been here before. This time, please factor in the lessons you learned."

But every time I hear someone talk about the "wisdom" of gut, especially for choices with true impact and no easy out, I balk. I know from experience—two experiences, in fact—just how inadequate gut can be as a meaningful and consistent guide.

The first experience occurred when I was twenty-one and, pounding the pavement in search of a journalism job, I ended up in Kansas City for an interview. It was 7 PM by the time I left the newspaper offices to walk back to my hotel, and an hour later when I finally admitted to myself that I was completely lost in the wrong part of town. Just then, a hefty, middle-aged man wearing a cowboy hat pulled up beside me in a white Cadillac. "I can tell you're not from here," he said. "Let me help you."

Like most young women, I had spent my life being told that getting into the car with a strange man without a Good Housekeeping Seal of Approval tattooed on his forehead was a form of suicide. But on that day, I took one look at this particular fellow's goofy, gap-toothed smile and hopped in the front seat. The happy ending of this story is that I had a lovely ride back to the front door of my hotel, during which I learned all about my pleasant companion's perfect wife, children, and grandchildren.

As we said goodbye, I thanked him for his hospitality and then, almost as an apology, offered, "I can't believe I took a ride with you."

"You know what?" he replied. "Neither can I."

Fast-forward two years. Once again, I was lost, except this time in Miami, where I had ultimately landed a job. In fact, I was lost somewhere in the spooky maze of streets behind the Miami airport, having taken a wrong left or right turn (or both) on the way to an assignment. It was pouring rain and my car had died. This was long before cell phones, and I was desperate to get out of there and let the news desk know why I wasn't where I was supposed to be. I was literally crying with frustration when a man in a pickup truck pulled up in front of me and, braving the storm, sprinted to my window. "Need help?" he asked. "I'm on my way to the gas station about a mile up ahead, right off West Flagler. I'll give you a lift."

I took one look at him and thought, "*No freaking way.*"

The funny thing is, the guy seemed nice enough. He too had a goofy, wide-open face. He was about my age and even sort of cute. But something made me tell him that help was already on the way. In reality, it was another hour before a police cruiser moseyed along, called for a tow, and took me home.

For some time afterward, I was actually embarrassed by my split-second discharge of that would-be helper near West Flagler Street. I'd only been a reporter for two years, I thought, but what a dark and hardened cynic I'd become.

Then one day, hanging around police headquarters as I was wont to do for my job on the crime beat, I spied a pile of mug shots sitting on the desk of my pal, Detective Joe Lodato. I'm sure you can guess whose picture was right on top.

"Oh, Joe?" I asked, voice quavering as I pointed at the photo. "What's this guy wanted for?"

"Him?" Joe said, grimacing in disgust. "*Everything.*"

Now, from these two stories, you might conclude that gut actually works quite effectively. My instinct, after all, led to two correct calls. But think about it. Neither taught me anything. In Kansas City, my gut said, "Go with the guy." In Miami, it said, "Don't go with the guy." And I have no idea why. To this day, I still wonder if I was just lucky.

Look, I'm not denigrating gut. As I've said, it's perfectly fine for small calls, and many times, it's all you have to go on. But as a way of making cogent decisions in your life that you can explain to others—and especially as the means to a deliberate, self-aware lifestyle—it's simply not trustworthy enough.

ONLY ACTING HUMAN

And there's actually a neurological reason for that. As I came to learn in my exploration of the brain's workings, gut is often no more than an inborn reaction that can have very little to do with the choice we are facing in the moment, and quite a lot to do with the choices that our evolutionary ancestors faced on the African Savannah.

Here's what I mean. Evolutionary psychologists today agree that a number of behavioral biases were hardwired into our brains to ensure survival. In primitive circumstances, for example, we were "programmed" to freeze in times of danger, as predators would rarely go after dead quarry. Today, we still carry that deep-rooted propensity toward paralysis, even if "danger" is coming in the form of a tight deadline or a big meeting. Similarly, during the earliest days of civilization, to break with your tribe and go it alone spelled extinction. As a result, people continue to have trouble bucking majority rule and consensus. Many of us have gone along with a terrible idea just because it felt awkward to contradict friends, colleagues, or even the status quo. In doing so, we were only acting human.

10-10-10 cannot erase the ingrained neurological biases that our brains developed to protect our species over the course of millions of years. But it can tame them; indeed, it can reframe them for the times in which we live.

Take how our minds process advice. When you have a problem, you may think you hear input from your wacky aunt, brainy boss, and too-young-to-know-anything son using an "educated" brain that sorts out who's giving you the most credible contribution. But studies in psychology would prove you wrong. There seems to be general consensus among scientists that several ingrained biases undermine our ability to sort out good advice from bad. We tend, for instance, to give the most credence to the last and first pieces of information we've heard and discount what we've learned in between, regardless of the information's veracity or relevance. Some cognitive psychologists also believe that we have a strong inborn tendency to believe the information we have heard the most times and give more weight to information from people we like and minimize information from people we don't.

10-10-10 interferes with such selective information "deafness." Your brain may want you to ignore something you heard two weeks ago or a comment delivered by a grumpy old neighbor. The discipline of the process won't let you. And 10-10-10 won't let you buy into information you've heard over and over again, either, because by definition, it "requires" you to test facts and assumptions.

LISTENING WITH OPEN EARS

For many years, Paula had struggled with her older son's rebellious behavior. A drinker, smoker, and all-around rabble-rouser, Kenny had two misdemeanor arrests by the time he was seventeen. But a chance meeting with an old friend in the military landed Kenny in a recruiting office, and he ended up enlisting himself. Within a year, Kenny was a changed man, Paula told me, responsible and mature. "He became an adult," she said.

With Kenny stationed in North Carolina, Paula could finally exhale. But not for long. One day, her younger son—a tenth grader nicknamed Hooper—received a report card filled with Cs and Ds. Paula was shocked. Hooper was her "easy" child—good enough at school, crazy about basketball, never a problem at home. She quickly met with school officials, and they seemed mystified as well. Hooper, they said, seemed to have "fallen off a cliff."

Paula and her husband, Jim, tried to get to the bottom of the problem, but Hooper would barely answer their questions. He did tell them that he hated his math teacher because his math teacher hated him. He assured his parents that not making the basketball team had nothing to do with his mood, and everything would be better if he just changed schools.

Paula ricocheted in every direction about what to do while Hooper continued to plead his case. His guidance counselor agreed that a change might be good. Jim, however, worried that taking Hooper out of school would only teach him how to run away from problems. On the other hand, neither he nor Paula wanted to keep Hooper in an environment that was making him miserable.

Somewhere in the middle of the mess, Paula had a short meeting with Hooper's math teacher, and she instantly understood why Hooper disliked him so much. He was stern-faced, impatient, and obviously not interested in engaging in the kinds of niceties that preceded most parent-teacher conferences. "Your son is depressed," he told Paula within a minute of meeting her. "He needs a doctor and he probably needs a prescription." Paula left the meeting so enraged by the teacher's audacity—he didn't even know Hooper!—that she found herself unable to repeat his comments to anyone, including her husband.

A dismal Christmas came and went, and when vacation was over, Hooper refused to return to school. Paula was looking for an opening in local parochial schools when a friend suggested she try conducting a 10-10-10 analysis. Feeling at her wits' end, she agreed.

Paula framed her dilemma as, "Should Hooper change schools?"

In ten minutes, she reasoned, removing Hooper from the source of his misery would be like taking a giant thorn out of her family's side.

The ten-month scenario was more confusing. Maybe changing schools would improve Hooper's behavior, and all would be well again. But what would she do if it wasn't?

For weeks, Paula had been fixated on advice from the principal and her husband. Suddenly, however, she found she could no longer tune out another voice—that of the math teacher. What would happen, she wondered, if she considered the prospect that Hooper was struggling with something more significant, something without an easy fix, like depression? How then would her thinking change?

All at once, Paula knew she could not make a decision about Hooper without gathering more information, no matter how upsetting it might be. She called her pediatrician for a referral, and within days Hooper had an appointment with a psychologist.

Hooper's diagnosis of depression ultimately filled Paula with relief—and gratitude. With its emphasis on testing assumptions and considering every possible option no matter what its source, 10-10-10 had compelled her to open her mind to hearing advice from a person she'd wanted to ignore. The process didn't let her.

Today, with Kenny stationed in Iraq, Paula is hardly without worries. But Hooper, now the manager of the school basketball team and a solid B-student, is not one of them. "Jim and I call Hooper our 'rebound boy,'" Paula told me recently. "I guess we have two of those."

KNEE DEEP IN THE BIG MUDDY

Along with helping us correct for selective information processing, 10-10-10 also interferes with two other common evolutionary biases.

Most of us can probably remember a time when we've felt compelled to hang on to a hopeless project or a failing relationship. In a nutshell, such behavior is what cognitive science calls escalating commitment, or the psychological drive to cling to "investments" even when they're clearly not working. There are a plethora of books and academic studies on this topic, but my favorite is the aptly named paper "Knee Deep in the Big Muddy" by Barry M. Staw, a professor of management at the University of California–Berkeley. It richly describes our tendency to sink into an ever-worsening situation in order to preserve our self-image, justify actions already taken, or both.

Now, you might be wondering, if escalating commitment is so pointless, why do we still fall victim to it so often? No one knows for sure, but social anthropologists have hypothesized that the world's early survivors were likely those who, even when faced with failures, refused to give up on activities such as farming, hunting, and reproducing. Natural selection rewarded such perseverance, and we can all be happy for that. But the neurological result is that we remain inclined not to bail out of our predicaments—particularly in high-stakes situations—no matter how disastrous they become.

By pressing us to ask, "What are the positive and negative consequences of staying in this mess over time?," 10-10-10 can break escalating commitment's gripping downward spiral.

"I CANNOT REACH THIS GUY"

Rachel, a thirty-six-year-old administrative assistant in Chicago who I met several years ago, is a perfect (if painful) example of how escalating commitment can get the better of the best of us.

Rachel is pure positive energy—smart, capable, and suffused with warmth. Her intuition about people, honed by years of traveling the world and working in successful companies, is ordinarily spot-on. But when she met Kyle, a handsome, redheaded contractor, her usual good sense soon started to seep away.

Rachel and Kyle's relationship started with a flirtatious conversation at the gym, and before the month was out, the two were seeing each other once or twice a week and spending hours each night on the phone talking about Kyle's work, his dream of getting involved in local politics, and the difficulties of his mother's ongoing battle with cancer. The conversations seemed so intimate that Rachel couldn't help herself. She was at the point in her life where fewer and fewer men were available. Was she finally, she wondered, hearing wedding bells?

There was just one catch; the relationship was completely platonic. Rachel convinced herself the reason was commendable. Kyle was too worried about his mother's illness to physically connect with a woman. And she didn't feel she could—or should—test that assumption.

Months passed. Rachel and Kyle continued to see each other often and talk nearly every night. Eventually, Rachel started making regular visits to Kyle's mother in the hospital, where she met and befriended many of Kyle's relatives. Yet not a single chaste kiss passed between the pair.

"Didn't you ever just think, 'Something has to be

wrong?'" I asked Rachel when she recounted the experience to me.

"Oh, that thought might have crossed my mind," she replied with a sardonic grin. "Like every night, I would go to bed thinking, 'I cannot reach this guy.'"

A year and a half after Rachel first met Kyle, his mother passed away. At the funeral, Kyle's cousin pulled her aside. "Someone needs to tell you," he said. "Kyle has a girl he's serious with—we all know her. Her name's April. She's over there." In the corner, Kyle's sister stood huddled with a pretty young woman who looked barely twenty-one.

With a terse text message that night, Rachel finally ended things.

"You know, I think Kyle really did love talking to me," Rachel reflects now. "The lie was that he couldn't marry someone who wasn't Irish-Catholic. Maybe I sensed that. But at a certain point I just felt so deep into the relationship, I couldn't pull out."

10-10-10, says Rachel, would have prevented her "stupidest decision ever" to stick with Kyle, by forcing her to see that her commitment to the relationship didn't make sense in any time frame.

To prove that point, Rachel conducted a retrospective 10-10-10 with me, placing herself a year back in time, before Kyle's mother died. Her question, as she phrased it, was, "Should I get out now?"

In the ten-minute and ten-month time frame, Rachel admitted, the answer would have been no. "I would have been willing to invest another year of my life in Kyle," she explained. "I felt like we had something, and there were not a lot of alternatives on the horizon."

The ten-year scenario, however, was eye-opening. If she and Kyle were together, Rachel reasoned, she'd be married to a man who was charming, but so fixated on himself that there would always be a piece of him outside her reach. "It was only when I imagined the distant future that I saw the real consequences of my inaction," she told me.

10-10-10, in other words, would have put the brakes on Rachel's deepening commitment to Kyle. Without it, she can only be thankful that his cousin was there to do so instead.

Today, Rachel is herself again; she just returned, brimming with excitement, from a trip to Honduras, where she distributed microloans to women farmers, and she plans to go back again soon. As for Kyle—she considers him a memory with an important lesson. "I will never not use 10-10-10 again," she told me. "I see it as a way to protect yourself from your own emotions—as a way to preserve your self-respect. What a valuable gift."

FUTURE SHOCK

Research in the field of cognitive science has also identified a group of biases that tend to trap us inside negative emotional states. We tend to feel, to put it very simply, that when bad times arrive, they will never leave, nor will our feelings around them. It's like New York City in the aftermath of 9/11. Some residents fled for the suburbs or even farther away, vowing never to return to the city's "irrevocably" marred psychological landscape, while the many who stayed predicted that the city would never regain its hustle and bustle. Of course, no New Yorker will ever forget that tragic day, but few would tell you now that the city isn't back. It just took time.

In our personal lives, the same emotional dynamic occurs. Emily, a woman in Texas whom I met through a friend, lost her beloved husband of twenty years in a car accident. For years afterward, she continued to wear her wedding ring and even had her late husband's name tattooed on her arm. Her sense of loss was so profound that she was convinced she would never look at another man, let alone date anyone. Is it any surprise, though, that today Emily is happily remarried? Emotions have a way of repairing themselves, but in our darkest hours, science has shown, our minds tell us otherwise.

Again, it's valid to ask why such a bias exists, and again, there's no definitive answer. Some scientists have suggested that strong feelings gave the earliest humans the psychological energy to fight tenaciously, even in times of great strife. But the point for today's world is simply that the tendency to believe that ephemeral emotions will last forever undercuts good decision making. Carnegie Mellon University economics professor George Lowenstein calls this dynamic an "empathy gap" with our future selves. We may know we will be around—working at our jobs, raising our children, running errands, and so on—in five or ten years, but we just cannot imagine ourselves doing as much in anything but a permanent state of shock and grief.

10-10-10 counteracts the empathy gap not by insisting, "Come on, you'll be better someday," but by asking us to *create* who we will become when that someday arrives.

A DREAM OF A LIFE

I met Lynne Scott Jackson, a marketing expert with twenty years of experience in the corporate world, after she had found herself in a position to do just that.

Lynne's dilemma had erupted shortly after she had launched her own public relations firm focused on the African-American market. "My dream was to build something very special," she told me, "a successful venture run by a working mother who was the descendant of slaves."

But a week before Lynne was due to travel to Johannesburg to work on a consulting project for her first major client, her parents fell ill. Neither one's life was at risk, but there was a flurry of tearful phone calls, each one ending with Lynne's parents pleading for her to come to Virginia right away and stay with them while they recuperated.

Immediately, Lynne's instinct took over. "Don't leave," her gut told her. "Take care of your family. That's the right thing to do."

An avid 10-10-10 practitioner already, Lynne used the process to push back.

In ten minutes, she knew one thing for sure: Canceling the trip would quiet her guilt. On the other hand, Lynne anticipated that canceling the trip would also let loose deeper feelings of panic and dread. Would her new client allow her to postpone everything? She doubted it, and even if they did, she feared making a bad first impression.

Lynne then moved on to an assessment of her life situation in ten months. Her parents would likely be settled back into their routine. But if she didn't go to South Africa, her company would probably still be struggling. It had taken her nearly a year to land the South African account, and could take months to find another.

Ten years out, however, the lay of the land shifted. Sadly, Lynne acknowledged, her father might be gone. But her mother, younger and in better health, would probably still be living. Health problems were sure to crop up now and again, and with increasing seriousness too. Would she keep flying to Virginia every time something went wrong? Even if such a step assuaged her guilt in the present, Lynne reasoned, it would undoubtedly deny her the opportunity to ever establish a successful enterprise.

And what of the ten-year scenario if she didn't cancel the trip? Lynne pictured herself running a company with perhaps twenty or thirty employees, the fulfillment of her lifelong dream, and an achievement, she believed, worthy of her ancestors' sacrifices.

The next day, Lynne flew to Virginia, not to stay but to arrange the ongoing services of a visiting nurse for her parents. Her consideration of the three time frames had opened her eyes to a solution she hadn't been able to visualize in her "heated" emotional state. She also called her brother in California, long absent from caregiving responsibilities in the family because of his military service overseas, and asked for his help. He quickly agreed to come east the following week.

Then Lynne left for Johannesburg as planned.

"By imagining how I would feel in the future—and how I *wanted* to feel—the crisis ended up changing my relationship with my parents for the better," Lynne told me recently. "It's so much healthier now. It forced me to set up a sustainable system to care for my parents. It made me get on the phone and bring my brother into the equation. 10-10-10 helped me get over myself."

Lynne's business continues to grow today and has led to a secondary career as a professor of communications at a college in New York City. "Without using 10-10-10 to tackle my dilemma," she says, "I might even be living in Virginia today, on call, with a life I didn't really want."

Instead Lynne is leading a life of her own making.

NATURE'S AUTOPILOT

When I first set out to explore the connection between brain science and 10-10-10, it wasn't long before I came to see exactly what Isaac Asimov meant when he observed that "the brain is the most complicated organization of matter that we know." Indeed, the main thing I know now, after spending two years grappling with behavioral economics, neuroscience, evolutionary psychology, and related fields, is that I am not alone in thinking that science, even with technology's great advances, will never fully understand the machinations of the mind. Asimov's "complicated organization" is as mysterious as it is wondrous.

Yet, science does know enough about the human brain to begin to explain how it makes decisions, both for better and for worse. And as I came to better understand that process myself, I was reminded of my old friend Fyodor Dostoevsky again, who once said, "It is not the brain that matters, but that which guides it—the character, the heart, the generosity, the new ideas."

10-10-10 can be one of those ideas. By having us methodically sort through our options in various time frames, the process challenges our deep-seated, neurological biases. It forces us to dissect and analyze what we're deciding and why, and it pushes us to empathize with who we might become. 10-10-10 disengages our decision making from nature's autopilot.

We will never, of course, be able to banish gut instinct from our lives. Some dilemmas are so complex and stressful that they resist our most disciplined and rigorous thinking.

But if you seek a new life of clarity and intention, then your brain sometimes needs an intervention on its own behalf to overcome the all-too-human proclivity to act without deliberation.

10-10-10 spurs us to deliberate, then act.

It gives us decisions we can trust.

CHAPTER THREE

Authentic at Last

The Values Equation of 10-10-10

So far in this book, I've mentioned "values" a mere five times. Mere because, when it comes to getting the most out of 10-10-10, that number hardly does the subject justice.

Without values, 10-10-10 is a device for surfacing decision alternatives, and far be it from me to knock it for that.

But it is with values as an integral part of the process that 10-10-10 truly becomes transformative, allowing us to live in sync with our authentic dreams, hopes, and beliefs. That's why whenever I hear people talking about their decisions—and especially when I work with people using 10-10-10—I often end up proselytizing about the overwhelming, undeniable, Holy Cow importance of bringing values into the mix.

I can't help myself.

You see, back in my youth—OK, up until I was nearly thirty—I thought that most everyone held the same guiding moral beliefs and abided by the same fundamental operating principles: Do Unto Others, Love Thy Neighbor, that kind of thing. I also assumed that most people eventually came around to the same basic list of priorities in life: health, family, happiness, achievement, financial security, and some right-feeling balance among them all. Simply put, I thought values were so generic that I generally tuned out anyone who tried to tell me otherwise.

Then one day during my second year of business school, a classmate bounded up to me on the quad to invite me to a party at his dorm that night. For a long moment, I just stared at him.

"Don't we have an industrial marketing exam tomorrow?" I finally managed to ask in a tone that could only be described as "withering."

He rolled his eyes. "I'll take that as a no," he said.

"I mean—the semester isn't over yet," I piled on.

"It's May, Suzy," he groaned back. "Everyone has a job locked up by now, including you."

"But there are still two weeks until grades are due!" I cried.

My classmate shook his head sadly. "You know what?" he said. "You just don't value fun."

And then he bounded away, leaving me floored.

It was a chilling revelation, and one that in time prompted me to look long and hard at why I was always working, working, working. The answer, it turned out, had a little something to do with my unusual Sicilian grandmother, but a lot more to do with something I now call the "Big Black Hole," a condition that results from a lack of values awareness. More common than you might think, the Big Black Hole manifests itself as a gaping emotional void at the center of our lives, begging to be filled with activities, commitments, children, studying—whatever busyness will mask the emptiness.

Thanks to 10-10-10, both my Big Black Hole and aversion to fun are now long gone.

And so too is my haziness around values.

Today, I can finally say that I understand my values, in all their ungeneric glory. More important, my hope is that by the end of this chapter, you too will have a sharper and more meaningful understanding of your own. Your 10-10-10 decisions will be far better—and truer—for it.

THE CATALYST WITHIN

As I've taken 10-10-10 on the road over the past few years, I've discovered that while plenty of people know their values cold, just as many are like me before my conversion experience on the quad. They may sense their values; they may intuit them. But they can't state them with any real nuance—let alone use them to make decisions.

Fortunately, the 10-10-10 process itself can be an effective catalyst for values identification, as it was for Jackie Majors, a woman from California who first wrote me in 2006 after my *O* magazine article about 10-10-10 was published.

Jackie's dilemma had been long in the making, but it came to a head when her six-year-old daughter, Leah, brought home a school project—a collection of biographies she'd written about her family. On the page about

Leah's grandmother, who cared for her while Jackie worked sixty hours a week as a corporate vice president, Leah had scrawled four exuberant paragraphs. Similarly, she had covered the page about her father, a teacher, with effusive praise and a detailed description of his pitching and catching lessons every day after school.

On Jackie's page, the entry read: "My mom travels a lot. My mom plans birthday parties when she's in town."

Later that night, with the children in bed, Jackie found herself fighting back tears. Should she quit her job, she wondered, or was there another solution to the torment she was feeling? Her thoughts scrambled, Jackie suddenly remembered that she had my article about 10-10-10 in her briefcase; a colleague had given it to her earlier in the week, with the gentle admonishment, "Your life is too crazy. You need this."

Jackie pulled out the article and started to read. And as she did, the dam broke, and the tears began. "I saw myself in every sentence," Jackie recalls, "conflicted, running every which way, never totally happy. I just sobbed."

For an hour or more, pen to paper, Jackie struggled to sort out her options and their consequences. But she kept coming up against a wall. "Finally," she told me later, "it occurred to me that I couldn't figure out what I wanted to do or what it would mean until I knew what I wanted from life."

She found a new piece of paper, wrote VALUES at the top, and immediately, the words started flowing:

"I want to wake the girls up every morning and put them to bed every night."

"I want to get off the money train. It's not the life I want to look back on twenty years from now."

"I still want to work. I'm wired that way. But my work can't control me."

"I love the house we're in."

"I don't want my worth to just come from my salary."

Jackie laughs now, remembering the experience. "Imagine, an executive like me, running a business, managing clients, developing staff, didn't have any idea of her real values. I sure wasn't living by them. I realized that night that I had sold my soul."

It took Jackie six months to plan her exit from the company, train a successor, and line up a new, more flexible job for herself. The week before she left, she prepared a stack of slides to explain her 10-10-10 decision to her direct reports. "I wanted them to know what I was doing wasn't arbitrary," she told me. "I was making the decision based on my values."

These days, Jackie works forty hours a week at a non-profit organization close to home. She makes the girls breakfast and dinner, and attends all seven innings of their softball games.

None of this is to say that Jackie's life is now perfect. With her new job, Jackie took a reduction in pay, and her family has had to cut back on some of its familiar extras. And Jackie will tell you, too, that she sometimes misses the challenge and fast pace of the corporate world.

But would she go back?

Not a chance. At last, she owns her soul—and her life.

TIME MAY CHANGE ME

Jackie's values evolved with her circumstances, and that's certainly not unusual. We all know a certified Party Animal who, upon seeing his baby's first smile, became the kind of doting dad who wouldn't dream of going out on a Saturday night. And we've all seen our own values adjust with seminal experiences, like the death of a parent, a divorce, or a new job that opens our eyes to what we can achieve if we only try.

Along with identifying our values, one of the great advantages of 10-10-10 is that the process often reveals to us *how* and *why* our values have shifted, not to mention helps us explain them to those they affect.

Melanie, an editor I met at a party not long ago, was brought up in a home of musicians. Her parents both played violin with a city orchestra, and her brother, who grew up playing piano competitively, is now a conductor in Europe. Melanie's instrument was the flute, and although she stopped practicing daily after her son was born, she never stopped loving the elegance of the classical form. Her son Ian seemed to inherit her devotion, and by seven, he was playing Mozart and Brahms on the cello.

But when Ian turned eleven, he asked Melanie for a drum set. The request launched a yearlong battle, with Ian pleading and Melanie refusing to budge.

After our meeting, however, Melanie decided to 10-10-10 the question of whether she should buy Ian a drum set for his next birthday. Her first step was to take a quick pulse check of her values.

All her life, she had spurned modern music. But why, she asked herself, was she being so rigid? What harm would occur if she opened it up to accommodate for changing needs and circumstances?

With that question, Melanie's 10-10-10 came quickly.

In ten minutes, amending her value from "classical music" to "all music"—or even changing her value to "finding common ground with Ian through music"—would mean Ian would be able to experience music just as she did, passionately. And the same held true for ten months and ten years.

By contrast, if she held on to her old value, she might turn Ian off to music—and to her—for the indefinite future.

On Ian's birthday, not only did Melanie surprise him with a drum set, but drum lessons as well. And to explain why, she walked him through her 10-10-10 decision. "That was the best part," she told me. "It restored a connection between us."

Just as important, Melanie found she had a new value—acknowledging, respecting, and enjoying her son's authentic interests.

A VALUES EXCAVATION

You don't have to wait for a 10-10-10 dilemma to discover your values or how they are changing, however.

For a quick assessment, you can ask your friends and family for guidance. After all, they've seen you in action for years, and your behaviors over time have surely shown them who you are and what you care about.

I've also found that the widely available "Proust Questionnaire," created by the French memoirist Marcel Proust more than a century ago, includes an array of excellent, values-excavating prompts, from "What is your favorite virtue?" to "What is your motto?" to "If you were not yourself, who would you want to be?" But my favorites of all are, "What is your idea of happiness?" and "What is your idea of misery?" If you answer honestly and expansively, those two simple queries can reveal quite a lot about your beliefs, hopes, and dreams.

And then there's my own values "questionnaire," which I developed about five years ago after finding that many 10-10-10 practitioners were having an easy-enough time coming up with decision alternatives and consequences, but getting stuck on the critical matter of their values.

My first questionnaire prompt concerns legacy: *"What would make you cry at your seventieth birthday?"*

This question, I've found, often gets right to the heart of a person's über-hopes; it reveals the size and shape of the footprint we want to leave behind. I have a friend, for example, who took less than a second to answer, "Knowing that my obituary wasn't going to appear on the front page of the *New York Times*. That would kill me on the spot!" He was laughing, but as we talked, I learned that his utmost goal in life was to achieve the wealth and renown of his stepfather. It also explained why he was so frustrated with his current lot in life, a high-paying but low-prestige job in public relations. He was experiencing a dreams-and-reality disconnect.

Not so for Shelley, whom I met a few years ago in St. Louis, where I was giving a speech about 10-10-10. Struggling with the question of whether to divorce an alcoholic husband, Shelley answered the birthday-party question with, "Not being surrounded by my whole family, all of us closer because we had weathered the storm." When I asked her what that reply suggested about her values, she began to reflect on her own rocky upbringing, and her sadness over the estrangement she felt from her adult siblings. By the time we were done talking, Shelley was naming "family stability" as one of her values, and "perseverance" as another.

The second questionnaire prompt I suggest concerns character: *"What do I want people to say about me when I'm not in the room?"*

To this query, I've heard everything from "That I run a great company because I'm smart and I'm fair," to "That I've raised great kids," to "That I'm honest and kind, but I'm no pushover." But the answer that has stayed with me for years came from Morgan, a former Las Vegas showgirl in her forties. "I couldn't possibly care less," she said with a huge smile.

Morgan was twenty-two when she fell in love with a casino operator thirty years her senior. They had a daughter but soon broke up, and Morgan decided to start her life again in New York, where she landed work as a model and tour guide. Later, with modest savings, she and her daughter moved to Paris, then Prague, then Madrid, finding adventure and getting by with small jobs wherever they went. With her daughter finally grown and on her own, Morgan is now trying on another incarnation, writing screenplays in Los Angeles.

"I think I'm pretty fearless," Morgan told me when we got to talking in more depth. "I love being free and independent. It keeps me growing. Some people value conformity; they think being regular helps their kids. I think the exact opposite. Change makes people strong." She lived her life accordingly.

My final questionnaire prompt concerns lifestyle: *"What do you love about the way your parents live, and what do you hate?"*

Remember Paula, the mother whose son Hooper was diagnosed with depression? When I asked her this question, she took a full, pensive minute before answering. "Well, there's a lot of silence in my parents' house," she finally replied. "I don't like that. Not a lot gets said. My dad's not one for talking about feelings." When I pushed her to identify something she loved, her face brightened. "My mother's a beautiful cook. She shows her love to everyone through food."

Through 10-10-10, Paula was able to translate both answers into values—and action. She wanted a home filled with openness, dialogue, and affection. Getting Hooper the medical help he needed was an essential first step in that direction.

DIGGING DEEPER

The three questions I've just outlined may tell you all you need and want to know about your values writ large, but if you'd like to keep probing, I've also developed value prompts that correspond specifically to decisions regarding love, work, parenting, friendship, and faith.

Love first.

Almost all romantic dilemmas, in my experience, come down to conflicts over the values of intimacy, commitment, and control. Sure, each relationship has unique dynamics. But when people get together, it's usually because they have a shared, realistic understanding of how their relationship will function and how much support and independence they need as individuals. And when couples break up, it's usually because their expectations and beliefs about their relationship are no longer aligned, or they never were in the first place.

That's why, when it comes to love values, I suggest you ask: In my ideal relationship, how much time do we spend together? How much of myself do I keep to myself, and how much do I share myself with my partner? What kind of compromises am I willing to make? Am I truly comfortable with a partner who's different from me, or do I need to be with someone who shares my values? You might also consider: Do I need my partner to be in charge, or do I want that role? Or do I value most highly a balanced "deal" where both partners have equal agency?

Remember, there are no right or wrong answers to

these questions. Their sole purpose is to help you assess your values with real depth and subtlety so that you can meaningfully apply them to a 10-10-10 decision.

As for work-related values, I encourage you to explore the matter of how central work is to your happiness and well-being. In this book already, we've heard varied answers. Jackie decided working was important to her, but not enough to supersede intimacy with her children, whereas Lynne determined she needed (and wanted) to put work first in her life in order to achieve her dreams.

For the purposes of making sound 10-10-10 decisions, it is also helpful to define what *kind* of work we want to pursue. Are we motivated by money, prestige, challenge, flexibility, or camaraderie? It's tempting, of course, to answer yes to all of the above, but it is a rare job that meets every criterion equally. To really know your values, you need to confront how they truly stack up.

Parenting may be complicated, but its underlying values tend to revolve around the answer to a single question: What do children need in order to be raised well? The answers range from tough love to unconditional love, from lots of activity to quiet focus, from wide exposure to the real world to fierce protection from it, from public school to private school, and perhaps most incendiary of all—whether children need stay-at-home parents or not. The challenge is to figure out where your beliefs land on the spectrum of possibilities.

The same holds true for friendship, where assessing our values is largely a matter of determining where our "voluntary" relationships fall in our list of priorities. I have an acquaintance in his late fifties, for instance, who would tell you he counts three people as friends. He'd rather spend his free time watching college football with his sons, playing catch with his grandchildren, and eating home-cooked pasta with his wife. Family trumps all.

By contrast, consider my old babysitter, Gladys. No one has ever attended more weddings or baby showers, spent more time on the phone listening to other people's troubles and worries, or more weekends helping other people move in and out of their apartments. She dedicates herself above all else in life to being a great friend, a sense of self that drives her choices large and small.

In a nutshell, that's how values work.

LIVING BY THE WORD

It is impossible—it would be wrong—to write about values without acknowledging the fact that millions of people strive to live by the overarching set of beliefs prescribed by their God. As one audience member told me after I spoke about 10-10-10 in Austin, "The values part of your idea is easy for me. I have the Bible."

But sometimes, devout people are a bit more stymied by 10-10-10. How can it possibly coalesce, they ask, with being religious?

My answer comes from experience.

If you're a Christian like I am, I say, you've certainly developed a few ways besides going to church that help keep you connected to God's word. You might volunteer with the homeless. Or garden to stay humble. Or pray during your headstands in yoga.

You can consider 10-10-10 another approach, in that it's a powerful means to make sure you are living in accordance with your values, no matter what their source.

That answer usually suffices, because most Christians, I've found, are already accustomed to blending their faith with the exigencies of the modern world. But if someone continues to press me about 10-10-10 and faith, I often refer to Colossians 3:17. In that verse, Jesus asks us to lead mindful and considered lives because doing so serves him. He doesn't tell us what to do in *specific* situations. How to handle the husband who seems bored, the boss who wants you to stay late, the child who's just been diagnosed with mental illness, the friend who stops calling. His teachings tell us how to live in general, which is deliberately, with truth and intention in every thought and action. If that's not in concordance with 10-10-10, I don't know what is.

In Proverbs of the Old Testament, God also asks us to live with patience. And that is how Ken Shigematsu first came to think about 10-10-10's role in a faith-based life. The leader of Vancouver's vibrant Tenth Avenue Church, Ken was preparing for a sermon in November 2006 when he read an article I had written. His topic that week was anger—or more precisely, how we can manage our natural propensity to feel fury, resentment, even rage. Ken wanted his congregation to understand that God does not ask us to repress or deny our anger, but to be patient with it, and with our actions, ultimately release it over to Him.

But how? In his sermon, Ken counseled his congregation that perspective is one of anger's most powerful antidotes, and offered 10-10-10 as a process to help in gaining it. When you feel hurt or pain and want to lash out, Ken suggested, ask yourself, will the source of my anger matter in ten days, in ten months, and ten years? Will it matter in eternity?

Along with Proverbs, Ken derives 10-10-10's theological support from Ignatius of Loyola, who was one of the principle founders of the Jesuit Order in the 1550s. When Ignatius was thirty-one years old, he wrote a book called *Spiritual Exercises,* comprised of meditations intended to deepen faith. One of those meditations concerns decision making, and in it, Ignatius suggests that when dilemmas arise, it's wise to step back and ask, "If I was standing before Jesus Christ giving an account of my life, what decision would He have wanted me to make?" Such a question, Ken points out, jibes with 10-10-10, in that it too prompts you to make decisions according to their carefully considered long-term consequences, often extending them to the eternal.

Ken continues to use 10-10-10 in counseling parishioners. "I think 10-10-10 acts as a great bridge enabling us to put things in perspective, whether they are challenges or even successes," he told me last year. "It's hard for people to think about eternity, but 10-10-10 helps with that."

FILLING THE BIG BLACK HOLE

Talking about 10-10-10 with people around the world has reinforced for me that each one of us has a profoundly unique set of values.

But I've also learned that not enough of us live by them. My friend Claudia, for instance, stayed married to an adulterous husband for twenty-two years because she couldn't bear to hurt her mother, who was a devout Catholic. She also struggled with her own values of conformity and reputation. "It's embarrassing to admit now, but I was really worried about what the ladies at our church would say about us getting a divorce," she told me.

Finally, after two years of counseling, Claudia's value of self-respect won out, and she decided to leave her husband.

As for the ladies at church, Claudia would tell you that they didn't really seem to care. They offered comforting words and then went about their own business. "I discovered that no one really holds it against you when you choose to live authentically," she told me recently. "I was trapped for too long. But I realized I had trapped myself."

Today, Claudia routinely uses 10-10-10 to make sure her decisions continue to adhere to her new values, which she names as "finding time to reflect every day and learning to trust again."

Most of all, she uses 10-10-10 to avoid the Big Black Hole that occurs when we have a sense of our values—even subconsciously—but can't find the wherewithal to live by them.

That was me, before my 10-10-10 epiphany in Hawaii. In those troubled days, I certainly knew my values, and contrary to what my classmate had said, I did like fun. I just didn't like it more than hard work or security, both values taught to me at the knee of my Sicilian grandmother. Married and divorced twice to the same man by the time she was thirty, Francesca Pilato raised her four children alone and sent all of them to college, debt free, from the profits of her own knitwear design business. Believe me when I say there weren't many other divorced immigrant women entrepreneurs in Rochester, New York, in the 1940s.

By her noble example, my Nonna's values made sense to me. And my own life experiences, too, amply proved that sacrifice and diligence paid off. In fact, one of the reasons I was so uptight about my classmate's party invitation all those years ago was that my employer had promised to pay for my entire second-year tuition if I graduated with a certain grade point average.

As time went on, though, I developed another value, deeper and stronger than all the rest. I wanted a good marriage.

And I was living a lie.

So I shoveled and shoveled and shoveled to fill the Big Black Hole at the center of my life. I threw myself ever more into my job. I had four kids in five years—and took two of them to Hawaii for no good reason. I hosted barbecue parties for the neighborhood. I taught Sunday school. I visited my parents once a week. I got a dog, and not just any dog, but a 180-pound mastiff. I kept a to-do list under my pillow and woke up at 5 AM to add things I'd forgotten.

When friends and family told me to slow down and ease up, I would reply with the joking refrain, "Desperate women do desperate things." But my behavior, beneath it all, was nothing to laugh about. My implosion in Hawaii was proof positive that I had been a values-disconnect train wreck waiting to happen.

10-10-10 forced—yes, forced—me to start making every decision according to my true beliefs.

Once I did, just about everything changed. My husband and I divorced. I also began to sort out conflicts between my job responsibilities and parenting with new success. As a result, my life began to be what I wanted, not just a picture of it. And my choices finally began to make sense to everyone, especially me.

I even started setting aside time for fun—my version of it. I attended my first U2 concert in a dozen years, and was so overcome by happiness during the band's rendition of "If You Wear That Velvet Dress" that I went flying off my chair, which I happened to be standing on. I replanted my garden and lassoed the kids into helping me sow and harvest. And every evening I made the time to take all 180 pounds of my dog for a long walk in the woods. Abby didn't stop to smell the roses, but she smelled the mushrooms, twigs, and rocks. She stopped to sniff other dogs, bark randomly at cars, and more than occasionally just to look at me, as if to say, "How's it going, girl? You hanging in there?" She is now in dog heaven, but I still thank Abby for her enduring lesson in proper pacing.

I value that now too.

In the coming chapters, you will meet many more 10-10-10 users, all making decisions based on their deeply individual values.

And in doing so, experiencing the joy of living authentically.

CHAPTER FOUR

Happily Ever After

10-10-10 and the Code of Love

Not long after my divorce, I developed a new Sunday-morning habit. Right after the kids and I got home from church, I would pour myself a cup of tea, lay out the Styles section of the *New York Times* on the kitchen counter, and read the wedding announcements—every one of them.

Usually the kids did their best to ignore me during this exercise, but one day, Eve, six at the time, couldn't stand it anymore.

"Why do you keep doing something that makes you so sad?" she demanded to know, looking up at me with her little hands on her hips.

"I'm not sad," I told her, surprised, because I truly wasn't, "I'm just curious."

I waved my hand across the sea of smiling photos. "Look at all these happy beginnings," I said. "Some of them will work, but some of them are sure to blow up."

Eve nodded solemnly, as if she knew all too well what I was talking about.

"Maybe I'm looking for clues," I suggested.

She nodded again. It was, she seemed to silently agree, a reasonable investigation, given the changed circumstances of our lives.

Nearly a decade has passed since then. I've switched to iced coffee, Eve is taller than I am. And I'm not looking for the secret of Happily Ever After in the newspaper anymore. The greatest achievement of my life is that I'm finally living it.

And it's all due to a code-cracking theory of love, a woman called Lulu, a mountaintop enlightenment, a great man, an instantaneous 10-10-10, and a pack of grape bubble gum, purchased, incidentally, by that great man himself, my own Jack, in a fishing village on Cape Cod.

Look, love takes a lot of things to get it right. It can be mysterious. It can be crazy. It can feel impossible. It can cause deeper hurt and take us to higher peaks of joy than anything else.

In other words, I'm not going to sit here and tell you that 10-10-10 makes love easy.

But I will tell you that 10-10-10 can help forge healthy relationships. It can reinvigorate them; it can pull them back from a precipice and make them happier, better, and stronger in every way.

I've already made the case that relationships can only succeed when both partners share the same values—or at least respect each other's. But let me—Suzy Welch, love doctor!—further hypothesize that relationships are far more likely to endure when both partners have a way to openly discuss three key aspects of love: intimacy, commitment, and control.

10-10-10 transforms relationships because it plugs right into that dynamic. By surfacing values, 10-10-10 gives one partner alone, or both together, a chance to consider momentum, chemistry, inertia, independence, conformity, tradition, or whatever is keeping them together or driving them apart. It can intervene at any stage of the love cycle, giving one partner or both a framework for understanding what is enduring about the relationship and what may not be.

TO THE PRECIPICE AND BACK

About three years ago, I received a call from Ajitha, a former business school student of mine. She wondered if I had a lunch hour to spare. Figuring it was career-related, I agreed and didn't give our meeting much thought after that. But when I found Ajitha across from me at a restaurant a week later, her normal composure and self-confidence seemed softened by a vulnerability I'd never seen in her before.

"Rohan and I were right at that point of no return," she told me unexpectedly. "But you need to know—with your idea, with 10-10-10—we returned."

A brilliant engineer, Ajitha had emigrated to the United States at twenty-two. She spent her first few years here studying in that field, but by the time I met her in the classroom, she'd been signed on by a prestigious technology company and was earning her MBA at night.

Ajitha had always struck me as the serious, driven type. But as our conversation unfolded, I came to find out that her prim demeanor hid another side—she loved to party.

"I like to *socialize*" is how Ajitha explained it to me that day at lunch. "I love the freedom and the camaraderie. What is life without friends?"

For the first five years of their marriage, Ajitha's penchant for after-work revelry was never a particular problem for Rohan, another engineer. He adored Ajitha's good heart, respected her mind, and appreciated her spunk. Sometimes he joined her when she went out; most times not.

But then the couple's daughter Laya was born. At first, Ajitha responded by cutting back on her nights out, from five to two or three. Her mother, who lived nearby, was also able to step in and help with Laya's care. But for Rohan, that solution wasn't enough. He started to beg Ajitha to stay in for the family's sake.

Ajitha didn't see the point; Laya was perfectly happy with her grandmother, she told Rohan, and if she stopped going out with her friends, the balance of her life would start to feel off-kilter. "Why are you trying to control me?" she demanded to know. "Why can't I have my own time?"

After a year, Ajitha and Rohan's sniping had intensified into a quiet war. They spoke less and less. They split chores they used to do together, like bathing Laya and grocery shopping. In moments alone, they both started thinking about a divorce.

For Laya's sake, they soldiered on.

But every relationship has its breaking point, and Ajitha and Rohan's finally came when Ajitha announced she was going on a three-day ski vacation with her MBA friends. Rohan's response was immediate and anguished. "You just can't, Ajitha," he cried. "Three days is too much. How can a ski trip be more important to you than our marriage and our baby?"

In the heat of the moment, Ajitha brushed Rohan off, but the truth was, his question was too disturbing for her to ignore. That night, after putting Laya to bed, Ajitha climbed the stairs to her attic office and closed the door. Then she sat at her desk with three pieces of paper in front of her and one question on her mind. Would she go away or stay at home? In her heart, though, Ajitha knew she was grappling with bigger issues: her marriage, identity, and future were at stake.

She labeled the first sheet of paper, "Ten Minutes."

The notation came quickly. "Ajitha = Sad," she wrote. If she didn't go on the trip, she reasoned, she'd feel awful about missing the fun with her friends. But if she did go, she'd probably be feeling too conflicted to socialize with her usual abandon anyway.

Next, Ajitha imagined how Rohan would react as she walked out the door for the trip. "Rohan = Sad + Resolved. Done with us," she wrote.

And if she didn't walk out the door?

"Rohan = Relieved, Confused, Hopeful," Ajitha predicted.

Ajitha labeled her second piece of paper "Ten Months," but this time, the "Ajitha =" equation came slowly. She stared at the blank space for five minutes, then ten, watching pictures unfold in her mind. One was of her and Rohan holding hands across the dinner table the way they used to, another of them bathing Laya together, chatting about her toes and hair and noises, just like the old days. Surely, if she chose to stay home from this trip and kept making similar choices about how she spent her time, in ten months, she and Rohan would have started to rebuild the foundation that was now crumbling.

Ajitha filled the space next to her name with the words "Connecting again. Better."

"I knew Rohan didn't want me to stop having fun," Ajitha told me. "He just wanted me home a little bit more. If I could bend once or twice, if I could even meet him halfway, he would be overjoyed, and our life would be back."

And if she went on the trip? Ajitha felt she couldn't be 100 percent certain, but in ten months, the second half of her equation would most likely be "Alone."

Ajitha labeled her third sheet "Ten Years," and jotted down "Ajitha = Satisfied."

The equation surprised me. "Why not 'Happy' or something more enthusiastic?" I asked.

"Well, I was trying to be realistic," Ajitha replied. "I figured that in ten years, looking back, I would still wish that I had been able to go out more. But I was also certain that I would say, 'It was worth it. My marriage was worth it.' I gave something up and we both got something bigger back."

"You made the well-being of your marriage into a more important value than your happiness alone?" I asked.

"Yes," she answered simply, "and I'm indebted to 10-10-10 for that."

Ajitha and Rohan recently celebrated their tenth anniversary with a vacation alone—skiing. Ajitha tells me they're thinking about having another child, and together have run the decision through a 10-10-10 analysis. "But we just don't know yet," she says. "We're still trying to think about the long-term impact on our careers. We just need some more time to talk it through."

A CODE-CRACKING THEORY

What delighted me most in my conversation with Ajitha was her repeated use of the word "we." It made me realize how effective 10-10-10 had been in aligning the couple, and in giving them a disciplined and dispassionate way to talk about melding their values.

10-10-10 had made their relationship bigger than the both of them.

And that's how love looks in the most successful relationships, doesn't it? It looks as if both partners love each other as individuals—but they love their love even more. They exalt it. They celebrate it. They talk about it as if it is the third force in the room, created by their merged commitment. They revere it and routinely and willingly make sacrifices for it.

I wish I could claim this code-cracking "third force" theory as an original thought. But in fact it comes from *The Good Marriage,* a book by family psychologist Dr. Judith S. Wallerstein and *New York Times* science writer Sandra Blakeslee. During the nineties, Wallerstein and Blakeslee studied fifty successful marriages and observed that, in virtually every case, the partners treated their union like a precious, separate entity deserving respect and nurture. In good marriages, the authors concluded, both partners treasure their collective identity more than their individuality.

Ultimately, that's the destination to which 10-10-10 brought Ajitha.

THE WAY WE WERE

The departure of a child, not the arrival of one, led to Jillian's crisis with her husband, Mike, a successful business executive who had once been the love of her life but had come to feel more like a stranger living under the same roof. For years, the couple had silently agreed to ignore the walls between them, but when their youngest son left for college, their detente collapsed.

"Suddenly," Jillian recalls, "I realized I had a very clean house and almost nothing else."

According to Jillian, Mike had never been hostile, just emotionally absent. He was physically absent too, and Jillian often wondered if he intentionally prolonged his business trips to avoid the muted awkwardness at home.

"When Mike married me, I was this carefree artist. Our whole thing was we were perfect for each other because we created a balance," Jillian remembered. "We'd spend long weekends sailing or camping, we'd always make dinner together. He'd come to my art shows. But as Mike changed, so did I. He became a big, roaring success at his company. I became a housewife. Sometimes I think I must have just bored him."

But when Jillian told Mike she wanted to reenergize her spirit by painting again, he scoffed at the idea. "Forget it, Jillian," he said. "Those days are over."

Crushed and confused, Jillian begged Mike to attend couple's therapy with her. He agreed to go—once.

The first session piqued Mike's interest, though, largely because he sensed the therapist didn't have an agenda. Instead, she introduced 10-10-10 as a nonjudgmental way to simply discover if common ground still existed in the couple's marriage.

As a first step, the therapist asked Jillian and Mike to define their values. "The usual things" was Mike's quick response. "Financial independence. My kids making it in this world. Respect from the people who work for me."

"What about our marriage? Where's that on your list, Mike?" Jillian asked, incredulous. "That's my main value. Our marriage and our family."

"There is no marriage, Jill, you know that," Mike answered flatly.

Over the next few weeks, the couple worked with

their therapist to imagine their worlds both apart and together. The sessions alternated between silence and acrimony and divorce seemed inevitable, especially after Mike admitted to something Jillian had long feared, that he had been unfaithful to her on the road.

But a breakthrough came when their therapist made a compelling point.

"You both loved your early relationship," she said to them. "You talk about it as if it were a close friend who died. What would it take to resurrect a new version of your old marriage?"

Immediately, Jillian and Mike began to use 10-10-10 to brainstorm how they could recapture the satisfying marriage they had had in their first decade. And just as quickly, they realized that reinvention would require a world of change. Jillian would need to start accompanying Mike on his business trips. Mike would need to embrace Jillian's return to painting. And the couple would need to overcome a raft of emotional obstacles to reintroduce themselves in bed.

They would, essentially, have to elevate their marriage to a priority above all others.

For Mike, the main impetus to give the plan a try was the couple's children. He believed he owed them at least one real attempt to save the family. And he sensed that he still loved Jillian on some level, or at least the woman she used to be. For Jillian, the motivation was more romantic. She adored Mike, still felt strongly attracted to him, and yearned to rekindle the fulfilling partnership of their beginnings.

About six months had passed since that decision when I checked in with Jillian recently. I could tell by her voice right away that things were going well. She and Mike were feeling so positive about their future that "not a day goes by when we don't 10-10-10 something we're doing," she told me. "We're always saying, 'OK, how will this choice affect our marriage in the near, mid-, and long term?' It's just like a GPS device; it keeps us on track."

I love that image of 10-10-10 as a tool to prevent a couple from getting lost. Because, even in the happiest of relationships, it's all too easy for us to take a wrong turn, or for life to take a wrong turn on us.

A DAUGHTER AND A WIFE

When Nancy and Carl met in 1987, she was thirty-six, a once divorced and once widowed medical records coordinator with a teenage son from her first marriage. Staunchly self-sufficient, Nancy believed the only thing that could go wrong with her life would be another man entering the picture. Carl, the same age, was recovering from a divorce, and described himself to anyone who would listen as a confirmed bachelor. But after a chance introduction to Nancy at a dart tournament in a local pub, he swiftly changed his mind.

Two weeks later, on their first date, Carl asked Nancy to marry him.

"Do you have a bank debt you need to relieve, or some kid you can't support?" she joked back.

"No, I'm just a lucky man who's finally met his lady" was Carl's steady reply.

The first twelve years of Nancy and Carl's married life together were nothing short of blissful. Sometimes, Nancy would awaken in the middle of the night to find Carl staring at her in wonder. She would smile back in wonder too.

"I was sure I had the happiest marriage in the world," Nancy told me.

Then Nancy's mother, Virginia, who lived on the first floor of their two-family house, was diagnosed with Parkinson's disease with dementia. Both Nancy and Carl were eager to provide care, but as Virginia lost her ability to feed and bathe herself, the responsibility began to wear heavily on the couple, physically and emotionally.

After five long years, Nancy reluctantly agreed to put her mother in a nursing home. But to assuage her guilt, she also decided to visit her every day after work.

Not surprisingly, the routine left Nancy more exhausted than ever. Her job at the hospital had expanded, and most days she couldn't make it to the nursing home until 7 or 8 PM. By the time she finally pulled into her driveway at night, all she wanted to do was collapse. Carl was patient, but even he had his limits, and the relationship grew strained in ways neither partner had ever imagined.

"I can't believe another marriage of mine is going to die," Nancy cried to herself in despair.

Then one night, as Nancy was driving home from visiting her mother in frustrated tears, she remembered reading about 10-10-10. All at once wondering what would happen if she tried to look past her feelings of obligation and opened her mind to other options, she decided to propose the process to Carl.

A few hours later, the two of them used 10-10-10 to decide if Nancy should continue to visit her mother every day. They skipped paper and pen for the exercise, instead sitting side by side on the living room couch, holding hands.

Their first ten came quickly—and presented a mixed picture. "I'll feel worse and I'll feel better," Nancy lamented to Carl. "I'm just so afraid of the guilt. But at the same time . . . I can barely breathe. I need a break. I'm exhausted. I miss you, Carl."

"I miss you too, baby," Carl told her.

"As for Mom, well, you know—in ten minutes, she will be very angry," Nancy hastened to add. "She'll hate me."

"Virginia is not Virginia anymore," Carl reminded her softly. "Nancy, you've been the perfect daughter for fifty-seven years."

"In ten months, I'm sure other family members will visit a bit more," Nancy suggested hopefully. "God knows they've offered. And if they visit Mom, I don't have to as much. Maybe we could begin to get our life back."

"And in ten months, your mother will have adjusted to other visitors, if she even notices," Carl put in.

But something was still bothering Nancy. "Let's talk about ten years," she said to Carl. "When Mom is gone. I'll want to feel good about myself as a daughter. I don't want to think, 'Well, I was fine until it really mattered.'"

Carl let Nancy think in silence for a long moment. Then she surprised him.

In ten years, Nancy thought out loud, she wanted to look back and think not only "I did right by Mom," but, "I did right by my husband." At the center of her life, she wanted a lasting marriage, a marriage that was greater than the sum of its parts.

"I love you, Carl," Nancy said with sudden firmness. "You *are* my life. I don't know why I only think of myself as a daughter when I'm also a wife."

The next day, Nancy didn't visit her mother. Nor did she visit her for another three days. And when at last she did, her mother greeted her as if nothing had changed. Nancy read her mother the newspaper and, for an hour or so, the two chatted about the weather, a few neighbors that Virginia seemed to remember, and the comings and goings of Nancy's son and his new wife. At her departure, Nancy softly offered, "I love you, Mom."

"I love you too," her mother replied in kind.

Not long ago, I caught up with Nancy as she, Carl, and other family members were preparing their annual Christmas baskets of chocolate-covered marshmallows and pretzels. From the lively chatter in the background, I could sense that the couple's life had indeed been restored.

"We had put our marriage on a back burner, but it isn't anymore," Nancy told me when I asked her if I was guessing right. And then, as if to finish the thought, she let out an affectionate laugh. "Sweetheart, please," I could hear her say. "Get your fingers out of the chocolate."

THE MATING DANCE

Now, I don't want to leave the impression that 10-10-10 is only relevant in established marriages. Just as often, I've seen it play a constructive role in new relationships, as they're being created and shaped. After all, the beginning of every relationship is always such a complicated mush of dynamics. First there's the seduction, or the "Hey, take a look at my best self" part, where both potential partners spend prodigious energy flaunting their assets, the way peacocks spread their tails. Then there's the investigation period, during which we try to suss out what's real about the other's "best self" and what's not. The early stages of love also include an element of imagination, where both people picture what the relationship could become, and just as important, envision how friends and family might react to it. And finally, there's the negotiation, in which the relationship's patterns, depth of intimacy, strength of commitment, and balance of control are debated, tested, and ultimately set.

It's not called a mating dance for nothing.

And I don't want to be a schoolmarm about this either. The early circling, weaving, flirting, flaunting, and checking-it-out stuff that most couples go through can be incredibly fun and exhilarating. But for all the thrill, the mating dance has its drawbacks. Too often it's mainly about posturing and maneuvering—with little sound thinking or values assessment mixed in. Nothing can completely overpower the rush and the whirl, but in the getting-to-know-you process, 10-10-10 can help keep both parties centered.

STARTING OVER—IN CYBERSPACE

The daughter of two poets who bounced from job to job across the Midwest, Heidi finally knew her first real home at thirteen, when her father landed a teaching position at a liberal arts college. The tranquillity didn't last. Two years later, her mother died from breast cancer, and her father, grief-stricken, quit his job and took Heidi on the road again.

When she was eighteen, Heidi met an oil deliveryman named Jerome. Following a brief courtship, the pair married and moved into a basement apartment on the outskirts of St. Louis.

Their first years were happy enough, but eventually Jerome's behavior started to become erratic. Some days he seemed to be in a daze, others he would shout at Heidi with the slightest provocation. For a while, Heidi suspected that Jerome felt trapped by marriage. But after two years of waiting in vain for Jerome's "moods" to pass, the couple sought a doctor. The diagnosis was adrenoleukodystrophy, an inherited neurological disease that usually strikes its victims in childhood, but in rare instances also afflicts adults. Jerome died seven difficult years later.

After a few months passed, Heidi decided to start over by moving to a small town across the state where she had landed a teaching job at a public middle school. She realized right away that she loved the work, but at the end of each day, she still felt loneliness and isolation creep in. Where was there for her to go to socialize? How would she ever meet anyone? As a well-known figure in a sleepy town with few single men, Heidi reasoned, she couldn't really date anyone from the community.

Late one night, she found herself surfing an Internet matchmaking site. Like most first-timers, the prospect both intrigued and repelled Heidi. "I can't do it," she told herself.

Or could she?

Heidi had spent her whole life moving around, feeling alone, and struggling against adversity. Now, a widow at age twenty-seven, she yearned for a real partner, someone with whom she could share the intimacy and commitment of building a life together.

An early adopter of 10-10-10, Heidi opted to use the process to decide if she should look for love online.

In ten minutes, Heidi told herself, online dating would be awkward, embarrassing, and probably fruitless. She would likely get rejected—and feel even lonelier than before.

In ten months, she would have either abandoned online dating because it wasn't working, or she would have learned to avoid awkward encounters. Maybe she would even have a sense of humor about the whole thing.

And in ten years, Heidi reasoned, she could be alone because she hadn't tried, or she could have gotten lucky and be with a man she loved. With few other options, online dating was simply too promising to pass up. She had to give it a try.

Six months later, browsing a message board for people who had lost their spouses, Heidi met a widower with the screen name "Been There Done That." Robert was forty-five, wry and gentle, with a teenage son and a passion for poetry. He and Heidi started emailing, then calling, then visiting. With each encounter, Heidi made sure to remember the values she'd uncovered using 10-10-10. She wanted to communicate honestly as she and Robert "investigated" each other. Having waited so long for love, she didn't want to undermine it by swooning or game-playing.

Today, Heidi and Robert are married and raising their young daughter in Robert's native Canada. Her 10-10-10 decision, she told me once, took her all of five minutes to conduct. But by reminding her to stay true to her values as she ventured into cyberspace to find love, it led to the life of her dreams right on earth.

PROCEED WITH CAUTION

It would be misleading to suggest that 10-10-10 always propels a burgeoning relationship into marriage. Sometimes, in fact, the process can reveal a relationship's fault lines, and in doing so, send a message to both partners to proceed with caution.

Blair and Andre made an unlikely pair from the beginning. When they met in college, Blair was an art history major whose priority was to find a job—any job—in the New York area so she could be near her aging parents. Andre lived and breathed science, and had already drawn a detailed map of his future: a PhD in oncology, which would likely lead to a prestigious medical research position.

Despite their different sensibilities, Blair and Andre dated exclusively for the two years leading up to graduation. After school ended, both found jobs in Manhattan, Blair as a receptionist at a law firm specializing in civil rights, and Andre as a junior researcher in a hospital laboratory. The relationship remained a slightly more grown-up version of its college self until, one day, Andre's boss offered him a fellowship at a Tokyo hospital.

"Pack your bags," Andre emailed Blair, "we're moving to Japan!"

Blair was stunned. Was this, she wondered, an oblique marriage proposal? And, if so, did she want to accept it? If it wasn't a marriage proposal, what was Andre thinking? Suddenly Blair realized just how much the ephemeral, undefined nature of her relationship with Andre troubled her. She longed for a way to discuss that with him.

But first, she realized, she needed to determine what she wanted from Andre—and life.

Blair had come to love her work at the law firm. Her boss was a former corporate attorney who was capping off a thirty-year career by taking on pro bono cases. Accompanying him to the courthouse, Blair had realized that she was deeply invested in the idea of social justice. She wanted to attend law school to pursue civil rights work, and her boss promised her he would support her application process in every way.

Another lawyer at the office, a working mother, had introduced Blair to 10-10-10, and that day, after she received Andre's email, Blair decided to use it to help her answer the question: Should I move to Japan with Andre?

To get started, Blair drew a chart with boxes for ten minutes, ten months, and ten years, and within each square she put the sub-labels of work, love, and family. She then prioritized work, love, and family as values. In the past, the order had been family-love-work. Now she realized that she had changed her ranking to work-family-love.

After that, the process swiftly led Blair to an unambiguous conclusion. She wanted to stay in New York to keep her career moving forward and to continue caring for her parents with the attentiveness they deserved. Not that she wanted to break up with Andre—she loved him and was bursting with pride about his fellowship in Tokyo. But if the relationship were to advance, he would need to join her in making its terms explicit.

"My decision was not an ultimatum; that's what I loved about the 10-10-10 process most," Blair told me. "I was happy he was going. I was happy I was staying. And finally, we were able to have the first real conversation we'd ever had about our future."

Would that future include marriage?

Blair told me she wasn't sure. "No matter what happens, I feel that at least with 10-10-10, we have a common language to talk about it."

Rather than ignoring her unease and assuming that they'd figure things out later, Blair had used 10-10-10 to determine what life choice would best fit her values. Indeed, she'd resisted the tendency to gloss over a sense of misalignment, simply hoping that something—the passage of time, a job, a diamond ring, a baby—would make the uncertainty go away.

It almost never happens that way.

A WOMAN CALLED LULU

My own first marriage was born out of that kind of glossing—and its companion, momentum. My husband and I had met in high school and shared years of common history but not a single common interest except the Roxy Music song "Avalon." (Sadly, I am not exaggerating.) Neither of us was yet twenty-five as we walked down the aisle, but no one gave us a word of caution—at least that we could hear. As my mother told me later, "You both seemed so sure of what you were doing."

To this day, I don't really know what we were so sure of. But I do know for a fact that when you get married for the wrong reasons, they will eventually catch up with you.

For whatever reason a marriage or relationship ends, however, 10-10-10 can intervene, instilling insight, deliberateness, and solace during one of life's most painful transitions.

One spring weekend in 2000, my husband and I took a hike up Mount Lafayette with three other couples and our kids. The air was warming, the trees were in bud, and the plan was to climb for a few hours, then have lunch at a clearing on the trail where our friend Ron, who was delayed because of a work obligation, would join us.

At 3 PM, two hours past the expected rendezvous time,

Ron still hadn't shown up, and his wife, Leslie, was frantic. "I don't want Ron climbing in the dark," she worried aloud.

Then, in the distance, someone spotted Ron running up the mountain, his heavy backpack bouncing up and down. Leslie saw him too, and suddenly she was flying toward him. "Ron!" she cried, her voice flooded with happiness. "You made it!"

"Lulu—I'm here!" we could all hear him call back.

I turned away so I didn't have to see their embrace.

A few hours later when we made camp, I found a rock ledge a couple hundred yards away and sat atop it, taking in the grandeur of the mountains as they glowed pink and red in the dimming light. They were millions of years old and would exist forever. I was forty; my life was rushing by. What would I make of my remaining time?

Another woman may have made a different decision that evening. But I felt I had no other choice. At my core, I believed that no one could live a meaningful life in a state of deceit. And I knew that my husband and I could never have what I so desperately wanted—that "third force" in the room, the sacred thing created when two people love their marriage more than themselves.

Up until then, my priority had been to guide and protect my children, to prepare them to lead their own healthy lives. That responsibility is what had always made divorce seem so impossible. But sitting atop that mountain, I suddenly realized that living a lie wasn't helping me be a good mother. What kind of role model was I? What could I teach my children about hope, tenderness, and connection if I had none myself?

My trip to Hawaii was only four years in the past, and 10-10-10 was still somewhat new to me as a process. But I turned to it at that moment for the most important decision of my life.

In ten minutes, I understood, a divorce would bring torrents of pain and confusion, as my kids reacted to the empty seat at the dinner table, the empty closet, and the empty space in our pew. I wondered too how I could break the news to my parents. For almost sixteen years, they'd seen me struggle in my marriage, and they'd pleaded with me not to give up. And how would I face my staff at work? I was supposed to be upbeat and confident. Could I pull it off anymore?

My thoughts turned to the ten-month scenario. Things might even be worse then, I knew. Reality would have set in for the kids. And surely, as with all divorces, a legal and financial boxing match awaited. I had never seen a truly amicable "division of assets."

Yet in ten years, I decided, I could finally be living a real life. I didn't have a clue what it would look like or where I would be. But it would be authentic; I would make sure of that. And, in my heart, I knew that my husband wanted that for himself too.

A few nights later, in a quiet conversation, we agreed to divorce.

My worst fears never did come to pass. My mother was very saddened, and friends chose between me and my ex-husband. I also stumbled terribly at work, trying to act as if my personal Waterloo hadn't happened.

But the kids never blinked. I took them through my

10-10-10 decision and they understood it as much as young children can. Once I even heard my daughter Sophia tell a playmate, "My mother couldn't take the pretending anymore. She had to make a decision."

Oh, yes, she did. And I'm grateful I had 10-10-10 as my guide through it all. My marriage would have ended eventually without it, but most probably in ways I would never have chosen.

A PACK OF GRAPE BUBBLE GUM

The day after Easter in 2002, 10-10-10 was there to guide my heart once again.

By that time, Jack and I were deeply in love. But the situation was complicated, to put it mildly. We lived in separate cities. I had just left my job in a cloud of scandal. And then there was the small matter of my four children, the very large dog, and the little cat. Where were we all going to live? How much time would everybody spend with everybody? What kind of family might we be?

These kinds of issues don't get settled in a conversation. They get settled with exposure and reflection. And so, that weekend, Jack and I drove with the kids to the fishing village of Wellfleet, where my parents' rambling old house stood empty. At first, things felt wonderful. Despite gloomy weather, we painted eggs, attended church services, and then sat down to a candlelit dinner that I'd spent hours preparing. Soon enough, though, I noticed the kids were getting a little—how can I put it?—frisky.

They weren't used to my having a man in my life, and they weren't so sure they liked my attention being divided.

The next day, I awoke with the bright idea that a long walk was just what we all needed. We piled into the car and drove to the harbor, but the outing hardly provided the balm I was hoping for. The boys were tripping and punching each other, the girls arguing about TV shows.

On the way home, I could feel Jack's hackles rising. I knew he was thinking, "I love this woman, but obnoxious kids are not what I bargained for."

And beside him, I was thinking, "I love these kids, but losing this man is not going to happen."

At that moment, Jack spotted a convenience store by the highway and swung into the parking lot. "I need some gum," he informed us. What he really needed was a break from the shenanigans in the backseat.

"See ya!" I said brightly as he exited the car.

I waited until Jack was out of sight, and then I whipped around and faced my children. My expression, they told me later, was "deranged."

I grabbed the kid closest to me by the collar of his shirt. It was Marcus, and today he is a fine and upstanding teenager—his school adviser calls him a "gentleman among boys." But back in those days he was a goofy eight-year-old who could spend hours on end speaking in a duck voice. It was his unfortunate fate that day to be within my physical reach.

"Listen here, all of you," I seethed, tightening my grasp on Marcus's shirt. "You don't think I know what you're up to—acting like a little pack of animals back there, fidgeting and screaming and poking each other? You don't think I know you're trying to scare Jack away? Well, guess what? I'm not that stupid."

As all four kids looked at me in a state of shock, I glanced back at the store to make sure Jack was still inside. Time was short.

"Get one thing straight." I turned back to my captive audience and rushed on. "I've finally found the one man I love. I've found the one man I was born to be with. And if you think you are going to screw it up, you're wrong. Jack and I are a team from now on. We are together."

I drew a deep breath, then: "I am doing what is best for all of us," I told them. "I am telling you the new rule of our lives."

And then I shouted it.

At which moment, the car door opened.

"Anybody want some grape bubble gum?" Jack asked cheerfully.

I released Marcus's shirt and turned to face Jack with a huge pasted-on grin. "No thanks!" I chirped. "Kids?"

From the backseat, there was dead silence.

Something you should know here. Two days later, when I told my sisters what had transpired in the car at the convenience store, they became completely undone. "You're wrong, Suzy!" they cried. "No man ever comes before your kids!"

"I wasn't putting Jack first," I corrected them. "I was announcing the terms of our new family."

At that point, I had been using 10-10-10 long enough to know and trust its power. That is why it was there waiting for me at the moment of truth, while Jack was buying grape gum. In fact, I made my 10-10-10 decision that day in almost no time at all. It required no paper and pen. I did it in my head in about, oh, three nanoseconds.

In ten minutes, ten months, and ten years, there were to be no wants and needs of mine or anyone's more important than the "third force" at the center of our lives—the greater sum of Jack and me together.

That choice was made.

"So, what's going on in here?" Jack asked, still perplexed by the new mood in the car.

"Oh, nothing!" I assured him.

"Nothing?" he pressed.

There was another long moment of silence. Then Marcus broke it. "Mom told us the new rules," he blurted out, neither mad nor defiant-sounding, just dazed. He was no longer, it should be noted, speaking in a duck voice.

"Mom says there's no more 'just her' now," he reported. "There's only you and her, together."

Jack burst into a happy laugh. Then he raised his eyebrows at me and I gave him a real smile. Not a word passed between us, but I could tell by the expression on his face that, on some level, he understood what had happened in his absence, and he was grateful to me for the gauntlet I'd thrown and, most of all, for my decision—deliberate, sustaining, and true.

There in the quiet, that shared and sacred thing between us drew a hopeful breath, and grew.

CHAPTER FIVE

In Work, Dignity

On the Job with 10-10-10

This chapter explores the power of 10-10-10 at work. But to save time, you can skip it if any of the following are true:

1. Your work doesn't really matter to you. OK, it matters, but not really.
2. Your work matters to you, but it's a cakewalk.
3. You've never had an out-of-body experience during a staff meeting, a performance review, a negotiation with a client, or any other work occasion, where you've found yourself wondering, "My God, what have I done?"
4. You have absolutely, positively no interest in the work decision that I kept secret for sixteen years.
5. Your inner goodness and lack of *schadenfreude* prevent you from wanting to hear about how I was fired twice.

If none of the above applies, read on.

Read on if you love your work yet sometimes dread it, or if you wrestle with your job daily but still want to wake up early the next morning and get at it again. Read on if you would embrace a process that would make your work more fulfilling. It doesn't matter if your work is washing dishes or running a corporation. All work is good work if it fills you with satisfaction and purpose.

10-10-10 will meet you there.

If only it had existed the first time I got the ax, back in the summer of 1975.

"WORK IS A DUTY, *CAPISCE*?"

The scene of the crime was the Cumberland Farms convenience store in Wellfleet, Cape Cod—the very store, it just so happens, where, twenty-seven years later, I was to lay down the new rules of family life for my stunned children while Jack went inside to buy a pack of grape bubble gum.

But back when I was a cashier at that store, I had no such backbone. Most sixteen-year-olds don't, of course, but I was particularly spineless. I was fired because I couldn't stand up to my mother. Clever and willful, she was such a force to be reckoned with that no one ever tried. Me included.

My downfall took just a month to unfold. The store manager, Mr. Antonio Scibelli, a sweet-natured Italian immigrant with a huge handlebar mustache, wanted me to work nine to five, five days a week—like any normal employee. Unfortunately, whenever the weather was good, my mother insisted that I join the family on our boat, hauling in the bluefish.

"But Mom, what about my job?" I would mumble from the backseat as we drove past the store on the way to the harbor most mornings.

"Mr. Scibelli loves me," she would blithely reply. "He'll understand. Family comes first."

Mr. Scibelli did seem to have a small crush on my mother. On the days when I made it to work—mainly when it was rainy—she would make sure to present me at the store, proclaiming, "Look, Tony, Suzy's here!" and his face would break into a big, goofy grin.

One rainy day, however, I didn't show up—my mother had decided the basement needed cleaning—and Mr. Scibelli called my house in a rage. "The store, it's crazy-busy! You get in here!" he yelled in his thick accent. "What do you think I pay you for?"

Quivering, I asked my mother to drive me over, but she'd have none of it. I considered running to the store myself—it was only a half mile away—but I couldn't bear the thought of my mother's reaction. And so, defeated, I stayed in the basement sorting junk.

The next day, the weather was still cloudy and my mother agreed to drop me off at work on her way to town. But when I walked into the store, my pigtailed head bowed in shame, Mr. Scibelli stormed over. "What are *you* doing here?" he demanded to know.

"I'm here to work," I volunteered meekly.

"You don't know *how* to work," he exploded. "Work is a duty, *capisce*? Work is not just—'I feel like it or I don't.' You're never gonna keep a job, you act that way."

"I know! I know!" I bleated in protest.

"Basta!" Mr. Scibelli shouted over me. "Get out. Go, go, go!"

I went, and I've been apologizing to Mr. Scibelli ever since—in my head. Even at sixteen, I believed work was a commitment to be honored. But I didn't live as if I did.

THE DAYS OF OUR LIVES

Sociologists have long held that work is a primary source of identity in our lives, giving us direction and purpose and serving as the organizing principle of our days. My own career as a business journalist has only confirmed that concept. In my years as a newspaper reporter and magazine editor, I spent time in union halls and on factory floors, at small entrepreneurial start-ups and in sprawling high-rise boardrooms. In literally every instance, I saw and heard that work isn't just what people *do* all day. It's who people are.

In recent years, my understanding of work—and how people experience it—has been radically expanded by an avalanche of newer data. Each week, my husband Jack and I receive hundreds of letters in response to our column, which appears in *BusinessWeek* magazine in the United States, and throughout about fifty countries internationally as part of the *New York Times* Syndicate. Even with our diverse audience, one common message comes through loud and clear. People care passionately about their work. It fills them with satisfaction; it maddens them to distraction. In sum, work gives people meaning. An elementary school softball coach once wrote us, "I've got friends who say, 'You're just a gym teacher, Bob, don't get so high and mighty.' And I tell them, 'Yeah, but I'm a *teacher*. I can change a life.'" A friend of mine counsels executives who find their companies in some form of crisis. She sees her work as essential to keeping the economy afloat. My older sister Elin runs a photography business focused on graduations and Christmas card portraits. Her work, she says, celebrates families; it fortifies them.

A Latin philosopher once said, *"In opus, maiestas"*—In work, dignity. Some things never change.

But in these intense times, dignity at work doesn't come without intense effort. Work moves blazingly fast; its demands are increasingly complex. It's constantly changing. It's never complete. You can give it your all, but it never seems to give you security in return.

For most of us, work stopped being a nine-to-five thing a decade ago. Technology is one reason; for better and worse, BlackBerrys, cell phones, and laptops make our availability ubiquitous. In the always-on exigency of the global economy, business never sleeps. And so more and more, we bring our whole selves to work, and our work into our personal time.

Now, more than ever, we need a process to ensure that our work decisions don't happen to us, but that we make them happen *for* us.

A VIRTUAL CONSULTANT

At work, 10-10-10 can play two main roles.

First, it can help with complex managerial, strategic, and operating decisions—from hiring and promotion picks to budgeting allocations. And second, 10-10-10 can be used as a tool to manage, teach, or counsel the people we work with. In both cases, 10-10-10 provides a framework for constructive debate and a common language to explore conflicting values and agendas.

In my experience, 10-10-10 works so well at work because it goes right to the heart of work's fundamental challenge. No matter what kind of job you have, whether you're an entrepreneur deciding where to manufacture a new product, a sales representative planning customer visits, an engineer selecting members for a special project team, or an executive opening a new office halfway around the world, virtually every decision involves a clash between the countervailing demands of the present, midterm, and future. Every decision calls for trade-offs and requires an evaluation of potential consequences across different time frames. At such crucible moments, 10-10-10 can act as a virtual consultant in the room, prompting us to gather data, test assumptions, identify options, and explore their varied consequences.

I discovered 10-10-10's consulting utility for myself when I was the editor of the *Harvard Business Review*.

Our goal at *HBR* was to publish articles that would, according to our mission statement, "improve the practice of management." Usually, we had a wealth of insightful, cooperative contributors to work with, but every so often, a renowned Harvard professor with an obtuse or otherwise half-baked idea would insist we print his text virtually unedited. And if we said no, the professor could raise a ruckus with the dean of the business school, the magazine's official boss and owner.

One day, a few members of the staff and I found ourselves struggling with exactly such a scenario. The offending contributor was a big kahuna on campus—I'll call him Professor Hampton here—who had submitted an article that was a retread of previous material he'd published in *HBR* and written in the kind of academic jargon we'd been trying to eliminate from the publication for years.

One of my colleagues had spent the day trying to negotiate with Hampton and was near her wits' end. Nonetheless, at our meeting, she argued to forge ahead. "We're in this so deep, we can't turn back now," she said.

"Why run an article that's not ready?" another colleague pushed back.

"We're running it so Suzy won't get a call from the dean," someone nicely suggested. "Although that's sort of what she's paid for—"

"Can we 10-10-10 this?" I interrupted when it suddenly struck me that the Hampton decision was just another dilemma with multiple constituents and varied consequences over different time frames—and inasmuch a perfect candidate for the process I used all the time at home. I quickly described 10-10-10 to the people in the room.

"Let's try it," one editor responded, to general agreement around the table. "The question is pretty simple, isn't it? Should we publish Hampton or not?"

The ten-minute time frame sparked a speedy consensus. If we went forward with the article, it would stall our efforts to change our brand image from stodgy to accessible. But if we rejected it, there could be a certain, unwelcome level of noise from the higher-ups.

In ten months, the outcomes weren't much better. Publishing the article would set a precedent for other difficult faculty contributors, making it harder for us to reject their less-than-optimal content down the road. And if we canceled Hampton, our bosses might still be so peeved that we could be stuck accepting an even less engaging article.

In ten years, though, the picture took on a clearer hue. "Who's going to be here a decade from now?" I asked the editors in the room. All of them raised their hands, and one immediately jumped in with an altered perspective.

"OK, hold on. We do have to kill the article," he said, receiving a nod or two from around the table. "Otherwise, in five years or eight or ten, we could still be sitting here having these exact same discussions."

"Just the opposite—we need to cut our losses and publish Hampton," another editor countered. "The brand is bigger than one article. Why cause trouble?"

Everyone looked at me. It was well known that I wanted *HBR* to modernize; I loved and respected the magazine, but I also felt that it could be too staid. On the other hand, I valued being in Harvard's good graces. I knew that even with my title and purported authority, I was hamstrung without my boss's support and the resources it brought *HBR*.

"Look, I think we have to run Hampton this time," I finally said. "If we want to change *HBR* in the long run, canceling this piece will carry too high a price. If we drop bombs, we'll become the 'enemy,' and that's no way to get anything done."

I'm not sure everyone in the room agreed with my decision. But at least everyone, including me, understood why I'd made it. And that's part of a leader's job.

GROW OR LET GO

Since that time, I have used 10-10-10 in countless other work situations.

Several years ago, for instance, I used it to prevent what would have been a truly dumb decision to fire my assistant. Megan LaMothe was a very bright Colgate graduate with a degree in math and philosophy. Unfortunately, she was also the Amelia Bedelia of assistants, making one blooper after another and redeeming herself only by the graces of her huge heart.

One day after Megan had been working for me a year or so, I was standing by her desk when the phone rang. It was my brilliant friend Nancy Bauer reporting that she had just received tenure at Tufts University. I let out a shout and literally jumped up and down for joy. As soon as I hung up, I told Megan why. "Let's send flowers!" I cried. "This is fantastic news."

About two hours later, my own phone rang. It was the principal of my daughter's elementary school, a rather ornery woman who just so happened to share a first name with my best friend. "I have two dozen yellow roses on my desk," she said dryly, "and I can't imagine why."

That's it, I cried to myself. I ran to Megan's office down the hall. Surely some invective slipped out of my mouth, but then, catching the better of myself, I scuttled back to my own office to pull my thoughts together.

In the short term, I knew Megan was going to continue to drive me insane. She was a whirling dervish of creativity and inexperience, heavy on the latter. But, I realized, hadn't I been like that once too? And hadn't patient managers tolerated and tried to educate me? Given her vast potential, integrity, and good intentions, Megan might very well be an improved version of herself in ten months. And in ten years, she would surely be mature enough to be flourishing in the right career.

So what did I do? Instead of firing Megan on the spot, I told her why I wanted to. Then I informed her that I would give her another three months of my energy, but if my investment didn't appear to be paying off by then, she'd need to move on.

Today, Megan is just about to graduate from a prestigious business school. She's still overflowing with goodness and creativity, but has become poised, thoughtful, and a complete stickler for details. Every time she tells people I am her mentor, I want to faint from pride. She taught me how to be a better boss.

THE ENTREPRENEUR'S ALLY

For people who are self-employed, 10-10-10 can be especially valuable—it's a way to bounce around ideas when you have few or no colleagues to bounce them off. That's no small matter when you consider the statistics. Companies with fewer than twenty employees number close to 21 million in the United States, and while precise figures are difficult to obtain, perhaps as many as 15 million businesses have fewer than five people employed. And even in these times of economic disruption, an estimated 2,500 individuals go into business for themselves every day. As unemployment rises, we can only expect that rate will increase.

Fortunately, the government provides some low-cost support services to small business owners, and entrepreneur groups exist all over the country. But 10-10-10 can also help individuals get their companies up and running, providing a quick and easily accessible process to examine tough choices and test the gut calls that so many entrepreneurs tend to rely on.

Joan began her career as a teacher, but after a surprisingly fulfilling stint as her elementary school's guidance counselor, she decided to go back to school herself to obtain a degree in social work. A few years later, bolstered by a loan from her older sister, she decided to make the leap into the world of the self-employed. She hung her shingle as a family therapist, and drew her earliest clients from among friends, former colleagues, and the families of her old students. Soon, however, Joan came to realize she needed a more steady flow of income if she was going to be able to pay for her own health insurance, cover the mortgage, and continue to maintain her other household expenses. She spent weeks trying to set up appointments with local doctors and insurance providers, hoping they would refer patients her way. Some did, but not nearly as many as she needed.

In a moment of exasperation, Joan called Mary Louise, the principal of her old school and a good friend. "I knew going out on my own wasn't going to be easy," she lamented, "but I may not even survive my first year."

"Vin started three businesses before one finally stuck," Mary Louise replied, referring to her husband, who had recently turned his first profit with an eBay storefront drop-ship site. "You just have to keep trying things. I mean, try everything, Joan. Try something with the Internet. That's the future."

Joan balked. In fact, she had been considering launching a small website for herself, but her instinct had been to spend just enough to list her name and contact information. "I didn't have a lot of money to spare," Joan told me of her early thinking, "and I just asked myself, 'Come on, who finds a shrink online?'"

But Mary Louise's comment prompted Joan to reexamine her assumptions through 10-10-10, which she already used frequently in her personal life. Her question, she decided, was financial. "How much money," she wanted to know, "should I put into marketing myself online?"

To conduct a thoughtful 10-10-10, Joan knew that her first order of business was to get some hard data.

That didn't take long. A brief online search revealed that therapists of all disciplines were promoting themselves on the web, not only by listing details about their training and approach but also with blog entries from patients, videos clips, photos, and podcasts. And when Joan looked at message boards and forums, she learned that potential clients were using such websites in the therapist selection process, and coming to expect them.

"I'm very risk-averse," Joan observed when we spoke not long ago. "But now that I'm a solo act, I have to get used to risk; I have to find ways to manage it. 10-10-10 showed me that it was riskier from a business point of view not to spend money." Ultimately, Joan invested $5,000 to design her website, even taking a course to learn how to manage it herself. The new endeavor proved so enjoyable to Joan—and fruitful for her business—that now, two years later, she is thinking about expanding her digital presence with a subscription-based email newsletter to reach all the new clients the site has brought in.

Those clients, incidentally, are enough to keep Joan's new business afloat for the time being, but she has no plans to cut back on her web presence. If being an entrepreneur has taught her anything so far, it's that you can never let down your guard.

You need to keep pushing yourself, with every tool available, to improve your business not just today, but in the months and years ahead.

NOT JUST GUT, GUT, GUT

Shortly after I started to research this book, a friend sent me an email. "I just Googled your idea," she wrote, "and I'm assuming you know about all the life coaches out there using 10-10-10."

In fact, I had no idea. Every 10-10-10 user I'd met up until that point was a person like me, deploying the process individually, or, in a few cases, with the help of a friend or partner.

But since that time, I have come to learn that 10-10-10 has become part of the toolkit for many people in the helping professions—teachers, nurses, therapists, and psychologists. Anne Jolles, a family counselor in Massachusetts, for instance, uses 10-10-10 to help parents who are having trouble letting go of their children as they grow up and seek independence. Meadow DeVor, an online life coach, uses 10-10-10 with clients who are struggling in their marriages and with work-life balance issues. And remember Heidi, the teacher who used 10-10-10 to muster the courage to try online dating? She also put 10-10-10 to use in her classroom, asking her senior students to select one big decision in their lives and conduct a retrospective 10-10-10 analysis, laying out what they might have done differently had they methodically thought about repercussions.

"You almost never *see* kids learn," Heidi told me of the experience. "But those papers were the best, most profound pieces of writing I got all year. Nearly every kid—and these were tough kids—had their eyes opened by the process. They saw the consequences of their actions, and in some cases, realized they'd made a mistake."

Kimberly Smith-Martinez, a psychologist in San Antonio who just entered private practice, frequently used 10-10-10 in her previous work as a counselor in the juvenile justice system. The teenagers in Kim's care were typically in the throes of crisis, and many were on the verge of dropping out of society altogether. To help them sort through the potential outcomes of their choices, Kim took the 10-10-10 process and made it graphic. Sitting with each young client, she drew a 3-by-2 grid. Above each column, she wrote: Ten days, ten months, and ten years. Along the side, she labeled one row "Pros" and the other "Cons," and then she and her client worked through the current conflict, cataloging its consequences.

The day I talked to Kim, she had just conducted the process with a pregnant teenager who was trying to decide whether to stay with her disapproving but stable family or move in with her loving but erratic boyfriend, a drug user. Using 10-10-10, the young woman ultimately chose to stay at home, reasoning that her family would provide an environment that would allow her to return to school after her baby was born. She would miss the company of her boyfriend, but in the end she decided that she valued the possibility of independence more.

"Realistically, I don't know what will happen to this young woman," Kim told me, noting that most of her clients had at least one family member who had died or was incarcerated. "My kids don't ever look forward. But 10-10-10 gives them a little glimpse of something they usually don't see—themselves in the future," she said. "It's not all gut, gut, gut."

TWELVE ANGRY MEN

When I was not much older than Kim's clients, I made a gut call at work that was to become my secret for sixteen years. It was only 10-10-10 that finally helped me understand and make peace with that painful chapter of my personal history.

The year was 1985. I was twenty-six, working at the Associated Press in Boston as an overnight shift supervisor.

What a joke. Not because a twenty-six-year-old can't be a boss. In family companies and entrepreneurial start-ups, it happens all the time. But it doesn't usually happen—and for good reason—in situations where the employees are cranky old union members embroiled in a longtime pissing match with management.

You can imagine how happy such employees were to see me. I had just four years of newspaper experience under my belt, and a Suzy Sunshine approach to the job that must have made them feel positively homicidal.

I wasn't particularly crazy about them either, with their snark and swagger. Since they couldn't take their resentment out on top management, some of them took it out on me. They informed me that they didn't trust anyone who couldn't name the Irish county of their mother's birth. They also wanted me to know that college was for rich sissies, and my college in particular was for rich sissy morons. At 4 AM every morning, they left for their "lunch" break, and a few of them regularly returned an hour later in a toxic cloud of booze. To my friends, I dubbed my employees, such as they were, the Twelve Angry Men. (There were, in fact, usually no more than five of them on any given night.)

Now, I didn't mind the minor hazing—being called "Miss Harvard," or being left alone in the dark now and again when they threw the switch in the fuse box. What I couldn't stand was the way a few of the guys would go into the bathroom about ten feet from my desk and pretend—at least, I told myself they were pretending—to "pleasure" themselves whilst shouting my name.

My supervision of the overnight shift was to last about a year. In that time, I never complained to my boss about what happened. I never told my parents, a friend, a colleague, or my then-husband. The first person I told was Jack. I was forty-two years old.

"Are those jerks still alive?" was his response. "Because I need to go kill them."

And then more seriously, he asked, "Why didn't you put a stop to it?"

I walked him through my thinking at the time, using 10-10-10 in retrospect.

First I reminded him of the context. In 1985, "sexual harassment" as a concept may have been floating around, but it had yet to gain any kind of traction. Most women were still gaining a foothold in the working world, and those who complained about inhospitable conditions were labeled whiners and fired or swiftly warehoused in divisions far from the real action. To get ahead, you had to prove you had the mettle of the next guy—or more. I'm not saying those conditions were right; I wouldn't want my daughters working in them. But they were the reality of the times, and like so many women of my generation, I had to choose my battles.

In ten minutes, if I reported the actions of the Twelve Angry Men, I had nothing to gain and much to lose. As union members, they couldn't be fired without a lengthy grievance and litigation process. That would leave me managing a bunch of men who hated me more than ever before. I could ask my boss to move me off the night shift, but unless I told him why, it would look like I was wimping out over the hours or couldn't hack it as a manager.

In ten months or so, if I kept my mouth shut, I knew I'd be back on the day shift, triumphant. In those days, you couldn't advance in newspaper journalism without working the overnight; it was a rite of passage. If I survived mine, I'd also have the satisfaction of knowing I hadn't let the bastards get me down.

If I complained, in ten years, I'd still be known in the industry as "the girl who couldn't take a joke," as the Twelve Angry Men were likely to deny what had really happened. If I didn't complain, I'd be the woman who had risen through the ranks playing by the men's rules.

My decision, then, wasn't entirely wrong, as the trajectory of my career went on to prove. But I paid a price for my silence too. For a year afterward, even while on the day shift, I constantly felt uncomfortable in the office. I didn't know exactly why; I didn't even consciously link it to the

Twelve Angry Men. Finally, I quit to attend business school. But whenever the subject of being a boss came up in class, I could feel my confidence ebbing. What did I know? I hadn't really managed anyone; my employees had run roughshod over me.

How sad that seems to me now. With 10-10-10, I came to see that by tolerating the Twelve Angry Men I had learned much more about men, management, and myself than I would have if I'd tattled or bolted. Today I even use the experience when I lecture at Babson College's Center for Women's Leadership. Working conditions for women have come a long way in the last thirty years, and most of my students will never have to confront what I did. But they surely will find themselves in dilemmas where a choice will have deep and lasting impact on their sense of identity. Don't make a decision, I tell my students, unless you can explain it to yourself, and to others.

And no, I don't use my first firing as an example. I use my second.

"YOU DID THIS TO YOURSELF"

It was October of 2001 when I flew to New York to meet Jack for the first time. He had just retired after twenty successful years as chairman and CEO of General Electric and was in the midst of a publicity tour for his bestselling autobiography. My assignment was to interview him for *HBR*.

Jack was known to be charismatic and opinionated. On the phone call to set the meeting up, he had made no secret of how much he disdained my scholarly journal. ("Never read the thing" were his exact words, I believe.) And so I arrived at his office for our allotted hour a nervous wreck, armed with a stack of meticulously prepared questions.

I'm not exactly sure how long it took us to fall in love that day. Nor can I explain why it happened. I asked Jack a question about leadership, and he answered with a few ideas I recognized from his autobiography. Then I asked about strategy, and the same thing happened. On my third question, he rolled his eyes, as if he was exasperated with me. "Turn that tape recorder off," he ordered. And when I dutifully complied, he asked, "Do you have a guy?" Flustered, I told him I was dating a doctor in Boston, which I was, tenuously. "Get rid of him, he's a bore," Jack announced, adding presciently, "He's not right for you anyway." Then Jack asked why my marriage had ended. His question was blunt, and, reflexively, it made my answer that way too. "My ex-husband would tell you I never loved him," I admitted, "but I spent sixteen years pretending I did and he pretended back. Eventually, we decided to stop pretending." Jack met my eyes directly and nodded as if he understood exactly what I meant, and then, to my disbelief, our conversation traveled to the daunting nature of marriage and the impenetrable mystery of love.

A half hour later, our "interview" feeling frighteningly close to the edge of intimacy to both of us, the tape recorder came back on, and for our final hour together, we talked about mergers and acquisitions, technological changes in the stock market, the role of human resources, and the quality improvement program known as Six Sigma.

Saying goodbye at the door of his office, Jack said, "You're nothing like I expected," and I answered, "Neither are you."

Over the next few weeks, Jack and I talked frequently on the phone—ostensibly about the progress of the article, but about everything else too. Politics, movies, my kids, his kids, religion, baseball, and the mortifying fact that I did not play golf. We had, it felt like, a lot of catching up to do.

A month later, I traveled to New York to have my photo taken with Jack for the Editor's Letter page of *HBR*. I was so (inexplicably) overjoyed to see him again that I was literally shaking in the elevator, and when I walked into his office, he bounded over to me, beaming, arms outstretched. Then we shook hands awkwardly.

That afternoon, we went to lunch, confessed what we were feeling and decided together that, given the circumstances, nothing could happen between us.

But a few weeks later, it did.

So it was that we created the perfect cocktail for a scandal—well-known, married CEO, a much younger woman, associated with Harvard, no less. The media had a party. But if they were having fun, we weren't. Even though Jack and his wife had periodically discussed divorce and had recently been living on separate continents on and off, there was no sugarcoating the fact that our relationship had started before theirs had legally ended. And because of that, and the sensation it caused, we had very regretfully allowed Jack's wife's privacy to be invaded.

I was also distraught over the awful disruption I had created at *HBR*. While my interview with Jack never saw the light of day, some members of my staff were livid about what had happened and how poorly I had behaved—and they wanted me gone. As one of them angrily told me, "You did this to yourself when you put your personal life ahead of your responsibility to the magazine."

Of course, he was absolutely right. My decision to have a life with Jack had caused so much turmoil at *HBR* that I needed to leave.

So why didn't I? Looking back at those four months when I hung on to my job knowing that I shouldn't, my best explanation is that events were happening too fast for the kind of attentive deliberation I so desperately needed to deploy. Yes, I had 10-10-10 in my life. I also had TV trucks camped outside my house. Reporters were calling my parents and showing up on my ex-husband's front stoop. A photographer chased me as I carried Marcus into the doctor's office for a strep test. Advice was coming from every direction—Jack, lawyers, colleagues, family, friends, college classmates, even strangers on the street. A priest approached me in a supermarket and told me he was praying for me. Running on a treadmill at my local gym, trying to act normal in the midst of the mayhem, I watched a panel of "experts" on TV debate how I should handle my dilemma. And then there was my gut, one minute shouting, "Quit now!" and the next, "Stay and fight." Amid all the noise and confusion, 10-10-10 didn't fail me. I failed it.

In the end, my boss fired me with the words, "You. Will. Never. Work. Again."

She must have been talking with Mr. Scibelli.

OK, I can joke like that now. But the truth is, I had

turned my family's life upside down and put Jack's family into the kind of spotlight they abhorred. I had hurt colleagues I once considered friends. I'd thrown a respected magazine into disarray. My firing was a disaster like none I'd ever known, and it was my own fault.

THE POWER OF 10-10-10 AT WORK

It didn't have to happen that way.

Much of the time—most of the time, really—work decisions can be taken apart, examined through a prism of values, biases, needs, and fears, analyzed piece by piece, and, with due consideration, reasonably resolved. They are, in that way, no different from the problems we face in our personal relationships. Every one of our choices has consequences, now and in the future. We need to confront those consequences with candor and courage, and only then decide what kind of lives we want to lead.

Starting at that little convenience store on Cape Cod, I've learned that work has the capacity to draw you into moments of deep confusion and conflict. But I've discovered too that work undertaken deliberately can and will fill you with meaning, purpose, and the better measure of joy. Today, much of my career continues to involve the exploration of work and the ways in which people embrace it, with their energy, creativity, hope, and passion.

Because in work, there is dignity.

10-10-10 helps you keep it there.

CHAPTER SIX

You Can Get There from Here

Charting Your Career with 10-10-10

Competitive strategy. Global markets. Monetary policy. Those were the kinds of weighty business topics that Jack and I expected to hear about when we first started inviting people to send in questions to our weekly column.

And we did hear about them, to an extent.

But we heard about career dilemmas more—by an order of magnitude. Indeed, to this day, most of the mail we receive still concerns the daunting dynamics of finding the right job and getting ahead once you do.

Jack and I try to answer many of the career questions that come our way, but what often stymies us is the fact that each one we receive is as individualized and values-dependent as the person behind it. "I dream of a career in music, but I'm afraid I'll never be able to afford a house and a car and my kids' education," a typical email goes.

"How do I choose?" Another correspondent worried to us that her desire for professional achievement was pitting her against her family's demands that she reduce her stress level. "Why can't anyone at home understand that I love my job?" she asked. "I want to travel. I want to work late. I'm not stressed. I'm fulfilled."

A WAY OUT—AND FORWARD

When career dilemmas become emotional or confounding, as they so often do, the rigor and discipline of the 10-10-10 process impels you to sort through the mix of needs, dreams, hopes, and assumptions that are making it so hard to find a way out—and forward. It's your guide as you weigh options and explore unknowns, comparing them to your values and goals. And just as important, the transparency of the process helps you explain your decision to yourself and any "constituents" who might be affected by it.

Carol Ann, a longtime real estate agent and a single mother, approached me at a conference in Florida two years ago. She was tall, blond, and dressed in bright yellow, with an out-there, ballsy demeanor—the kind of woman once referred to as a "great broad." Her only son had just left for college and at long last, Carol Ann told me with a smile, she was ready to have some fun with her friends instead of running home every evening after work.

Carol Ann's company, however, had another plan. They wanted her to relocate from Tampa, where she had lived and worked for twenty years, to their Houston headquarters to lead corporate training. The title, prestige, and significant pay increase of the new opportunity thrilled her. The potential for loneliness did not.

At Carol Ann's request, we started to 10-10-10 together.

In the ten-minute time frame, and even for weeks afterward, Carol Ann knew she would be elated by her promotion. She'd delight in the sense of achievement and the relief of paying off her son's student loan. She'd even be excited about finding a town house in Houston's buyer's market. "I love a bargain," she told me with a hearty laugh.

The ten-month picture was more mixed. "My job will be great, but my social life will be dead. I don't know anyone in Texas," Carol Ann said. "In ten months, the quiet nights will be killing me."

And what about ten years? Carol Ann paused before answering. "I'll have a nice bank account and a good pension plan by then. After the financial struggles in my life, I have to tell you, I'd love that." She sighed deeply, her ambivalence tugging her face into a pensive frown. "But I'll have lost all my old friends in the process."

"You'll lose some friends," I said, more as a test than anything. "That always happens when you move. But with your personality, I bet you'll make plenty of new ones."

"Probably," she agreed. "Hey, maybe I'll even meet a man." She laughed again.

Then Carol Ann surprised me.

"You know what? I don't want to be clipping coupons in the supermarket circular," she announced. "I want a nice, comfortable retirement. And I want this new job. It will be fun. There's no better saleswoman in the company. You can ask anyone."

Before I could congratulate Carol Ann on a decision, though, she reversed herself. "But—I just can't leave my friends," she said.

I asked Carol Ann if the problem wasn't leaving her friends, but *telling* them she planned to do so. Maybe she feared her announcement would seem to say, "Guess what, everybody—money matters more to me than you do."

"Do you think your friends are going to be mad at you forever?" I pressed her. "Some of them may understand the value you place on financial security."

A smile started to spread across Carol Ann's face. "I get where you're going," she said. "In a year, I won't even remember the day I told everybody." Carol Ann grabbed my hand. "I can't build my life around fear. I'm taking the damn promotion," she exclaimed. "I knew I wanted to."

10-10-10 was her partner in making sure.

Carol Ann's dilemma stemmed from a conflict between the joy of her old life and the promise of a new one. But there are three other issues that most commonly set off career quandaries, and if you were to categorize them, they would sound something like this: "I'm worried I'm in the wrong job," "I think my career has stalled," and "My work-life balance is driving me crazy."

My hope is that by looking at each one of these tinderboxes in turn, and suggesting ways you might think about them, your next career 10-10-10 will be more focused and informed, providing the sustainable solution that's right for you.

WHAT SHOULD I DO WITH MY LIFE?

When I speak on college campuses, I'm often asked how I decided to become a journalist.

"I'm not sure I ever *decided,*" I usually answer. "I just knew—I always knew—there was nothing else I could do with my life." As evidence, I confess that in fourth grade I started keeping a diary in a little hand-decorated book with a cover inscription stating: "I shall write in here every night to practice for my future." (Yes, "shall." How mortifying.) In tenth grade, I could name the newspapers published in every American city, and by my freshman year in college, I had a poster of the audacious Italian war correspondent Oriana Fallaci hanging over my bed. She was my role model and my idol; I longed to be her.

OK, so I missed that particular mark by a mile. But I still am, basically, what I wanted to be as a kid, practicing for my future in the pages of my diary.

And that actually ends up making me more of the exception than the rule. Most people, I've found in writing about career formation, ultimately discover the profession that feels right to them through a vastly more iterative process. They try on one line of work, then zig and zag through related areas and positions, until they finally land in a good place.

Unfortunately, that process can take a decade or more, leading to the somewhat ironic reality that you finally discover "what you want to be when you grow up" when you've finally grown up. For women, it can be an even longer path, as their careers often involve stops and starts and flexibility-friendly digressions due to having children.

That said, it is possible to expedite your career's progression and arrive at the coordinates you so desire sooner rather than later. But that outcome takes a certain intentionality along the way.

10-10-10 can be your guide. To facilitate the process, however, I recommend first considering four questions about your job. The answers should stir up the "data" you need to start making meaningful career decisions.

Does my job allow me to work with "my people"—those who share my sensibilities about life—or do I have to zone out, fake it, or put on a persona to get through the day? The key word in this question is "sensibilities"—the values, behaviors, and personality traits that make you feel as if you're among kindred spirits. If you share sensibilities with your colleagues, you tend to work at the same pace, confront each other about tough issues with the same level of intensity (or lack thereof), and tell the same sorts of jokes in meetings. I'm not saying that people with shared sensibilities are all alike, but they pretty much all like one another.

I will never forget the firecracker of a woman—her nickname was "Sunny"—whom I met through my family a few years ago. "When I graduated from college, all I knew was that I wanted a job where I could wear high heels and carry a briefcase," she told me. "For a country girl like me, that meant you'd made something of yourself." Without much more thought than that, Sunny nabbed a position as a paralegal.

Two years later, she was out of there. "It was torture,"

she recalled. "No one laughed at what I laughed at. No one thought it was OK to argue now and again if you had to get some issues off the table. No one even enjoyed the same kind of music I did."

"I'm not saying it was a bad place," she concluded. "I just realized it wasn't *my* kind of place."

Sunny's next job was in catering—at least there were no suits involved—but when the work started to bore her a year later, she quit. Next, to pay the bills, she took a position as a project manager at a museum installation firm. Almost immediately, Sunny realized she was on to something. She loved the creativity and camaraderie involved in the job, and for the first time, it felt completely natural to her to stay late, suggest ideas, and connect with clients. One promotion led to another, and today, Sunny has found success in the related field of aquarium administration. She wears a T-shirt, shorts, and flip-flops to work, and doesn't even own a briefcase. Most important, she says, "I love the people I work with. We agree about what matters. I mean, we just see the world the same way."

The fact is, no job or profession will ever be right for you if it requires you to work with people who don't share your values or appreciate you as you are. You spend most of your life at work—a point well worth factoring into any 10-10-10 career dilemma. You have to like your colleagues—and feel authentic around them—if you are ever going to have a career you like.

Does my job make me smarter by stretching my mind, building my skills, and taking me out of my comfort zone?

Without a doubt, it's appealing to hold a job where you feel like the smartest person in the room. In time, though, such efficacy can be a real career-killer. To feel fulfilled, you have to be growing.

Here's the catch: people tend to gravitate toward and stay ensconced in certain professions simply because they are good at them. English majors go into publishing. Math majors go to Wall Street. My own sister Elin, who excelled in science through high school and college, "naturally" followed the current to graduate school and became a medical researcher.

But aptitude doesn't always equal passion. Thirteen years ago, when she was forty, my sister finally admitted to herself and her friends (not to mention our parents) that she never wanted to look through a microscope again. She quit science and started to look for an authentic vocation. She found it in photography.

Changing careers was rough going at first. Elin apprenticed herself to experienced photographers to expand her knowledge and scrimped to attend summer workshops on lighting and technique. She designed flyers and sent them to her neighbors and painstakingly sought new ways to market her services to communities across Boston's North Shore.

She loved every minute of it.

I am delighted to report that Elin's business is thriving—and she is too. Moral is, if your career 10-10-10 involves a change of direction, don't just ask, "Do I have the right skills?" Ask: "Will I enjoy the challenge of gaining new ones?"

Does my job open doors for me? As contradictory as it might sound, you can be pretty sure you're holding the right job if it has the potential to lead to another job elsewhere. That's because careers, by definition, don't have dead-ends. They are comprised of opportunities that lead to other opportunities.

In teaching at Babson College, I'm sometimes approached by seniors who are using 10-10-10 to decide between two job offers. I remember one student, Kristin, who came to our meeting with a carefully prepared list of pros and cons for both of her options, and a look of total exasperation on her face. "I'm stuck," she explained. "One of the jobs would be great for me for the next year or two. It's a little start-up. The work is fun and the people are great. But the company may not even survive. The other company has a great reputation, great training programs, and lots of upward mobility. It makes much better sense for me in a ten-year time frame. It's such a toss-up that I don't know what to do."

I reminded Kristin that every 10-10-10 solution depends on the values of the person conducting the process, but that didn't seem to help. Both opportunities gave her what she wanted from life, she said—intellectual challenge, teamwork, and enough money to stay afloat.

I pushed Kristin to think more deeply about her career values. "Well, I'm not big on titles or prestige," she finally said. "I'd rather have responsibility than authority." Kristin, it turned out, dreamed of a résumé filled with stints at small ventures where she could have true impact, and hopefully a piece of the ownership as well.

"Which job opportunity opens those doors for you?" I asked, but we both already knew the answer. Kristin soon accepted her offer from the start-up.

The days of one-company careers are fading fast. So as you consider your career choices with 10-10-10, make sure that each job you hold at least offers you the chance to launch to another.

Does my job give me meaning? Every holiday when my kids return home from school and we start to select their courses for the following semester, we invariably end up in the "What should I do with my life?" conversation. And every holiday, I have to remind my kids that no one ever built a great career doing something they hated.

Do what you love, I tell them, and the rest will follow.

"Sure, Mom, sure," they brush me off, "but isn't biotech a hot industry right now?"

"It is," I try to tell them, "for people who happen to like biotech."

Look, the perfect job—and the perfect career—are only perfect if they make you happy. Something about the work—the thrill of making a big sale, the excitement of hitting a deadline with your colleagues, the reward of coaching a newcomer or helping a customer—just turns your crank. It feels important; it fills your soul.

I am reminded of the first real stepping-stone of my own career, my job as a reporter at the *Miami Herald*.

For an Oriana Fallaci wannabe, there was no better place to be a reporter than Miami in the 1980s. In 1981 and 1982, the city was engulfed in riots, as residents of the Overtown and Liberty City neighborhoods protested the jury acquittals of white policemen accused of racially motivated violence. The burning and looting were so severe that the National Guard was called in and curfews were declared. Then in 1983, Miami was besieged by thousands of refugees, most of whom were hardened criminals Fidel Castro had just released from Cuban prisons. Meanwhile, cocaine traffickers battled one another in street-corner shoot-'em-ups in broad daylight.

The city wasn't a full-on war zone, but it was close.

Oh, to be a girl reporter then! I remember wearing a bulletproof vest during one assignment, which in the greenness of my youth filled me with pride. As we were creeping into a cocaine-processing factory in Perrine with a SWAT team one night, a rookie cop handed me a revolver and said, "You may need this." Another morning I remember waking up to see government tanks rolling down my quiet residential street in Coconut Grove, and not thinking, "Help!" but "Hallelujah!" There was just so much to write about. Not all of it was exciting, of course. For many of Miami's longtime residents, the city's implosion caused fear and sadness, and for residents of the riot areas, the violence took a dreadful toll. But I desperately wanted to hear their stories too; I wanted to tell them in all their heart-wrenching detail. My job gave me that great gift and opportunity.

Nearly thirty years have passed, but Miami has never left me. The experience taught me what a career should feel like. And in time, it taught me too that you simply cannot, and should not, 10-10-10 any career dilemma without acknowledging the "joy factor" of your options.

KEEP YOUR NOSE ABOVE THE HORIZON

I have a friend who takes flying lessons, and whenever I express terror at his idea of fun, he shrugs me off with a laugh. "It's actually very easy to fly, Suzy," he says. "You just keep the nose of the plane above the horizon."

Careers are like that too. To stay aloft, you need to keep your sights just high enough.

And you have to pay attention—quickly—when your nose starts dipping. You miss a promotion. Your bonus is flat. Your boss stops inviting you to important meetings. In such cases, something is usually off.

Something is stalling.

If you use 10-10-10, the next thing you know, you'll be applying the process to a "Do I stay or do I go?" kind of dilemma.

As you do, however, it's all too easy to get caught up in the feelings of rejection, confusion, and anxiety of the moment. After all, almost nothing is as disconcerting as the sneaking suspicion that everyone is in on something that you're not. To overcome your emotions, once again a certain intentionality is required. You need to stop, step back, and make a pact with yourself that you have work to do before deciding anything.

Now, identifying the source of your stall may sound easy enough, but I've found that many people assign the blame for their situation to the economy, a bad boss, a scheming coworker, or any number of other forces outside their control. Extenuating circumstances may indeed be involved, but before conducting any meaningful career-stall 10-10-10, you need to determine if your own behaviors can be implicated as well.

The hard truth is, our careers rarely stall when we're performing well. And I don't just mean performing at expectations, I mean above them. For better or worse, overdelivering is what our bosses want, need, and expect in these competitive times. So if you notice your "nose" dipping at work, you need to have an honest conversation with yourself or a colleague you trust about your results. How good are they, *really*?

Unfortunately, we rarely know the answer to that question until it's too late. And there's an incontrovertible reason why. Most managers don't have the guts or the time—or both—to tell their employees where they stand.

I plead guilty.

Dave was the first person I ever fired. He'd worked at our company for many years before I arrived, and after I was promoted to being his boss, never seemed to get comfortable with my authority. As for his performance, it started out as adequate, but over time disintegrated to poor. He was political, divisive, and unproductive. Finally I decided he needed to move on.

Looking back, how could I have expected Dave to take the news sitting down? He had no idea it was coming—because I had never told him how he was doing.

The fallout of Dave's firing was a mess. He screamed at me in the meeting, waged a campaign through his coworkers to be rehired, and later threatened to sue the company unless he received a substantial cash payment. (Eventually, we settled.)

If your career seems to be in a stall, try to pinpoint the date and content of your last *real* performance review. Don't assume you're doing OK because your boss hasn't told you otherwise. And remember, don't conduct a stay-or-go 10-10-10 until you get the candid feedback you need on your performance. Only then can you decide whether your stall is reversible, or if a bailout is your only hope.

Along with problematic performance, our careers tend to stall for two other reasons. We have the wrong leadership mind-set or we're suffering from an embedded reputation.

FROM HERO TO ZERO

You don't need me to tell you that not everyone can be a leader, but if there's one thing I've learned over time, it's that most companies want everyone to *demonstrate* leadership qualities. That's why, if we start showing signs that we're not a person who can take charge—at least, someday—we stand the chance of slowly but surely being moved aside and then out the door.

And what does a person who can take charge actually look like? There's no universal leadership profile. Some companies want their leaders to be technically proficient. Others want them to have global experience. Still others like their leaders to have certain educational credentials. But virtually all companies know that the most effective leaders share one trait—they understand that success is not about them. It's about the team. Being a good leader means being turned on by the reflected glory of the people who work for you. Being a good leader means you honestly think it's more fun to see your people grow than to get your own ego stroked.

About three years ago, Jack and I received a poignant email to our column from a man who signed his note, "From Hero to Zero." A "quant jock" at a financial firm, his career had soared for six years, and along the way, his salary growth had never let up.

But then something strange happened, our correspondent said. He grew tired of just crunching numbers. He wanted to be a leader. And so, he asked to manage a department within his firm.

"You must be kidding," his bosses replied.

"They said I didn't care about my colleagues' ideas, and I never wondered how I might help them do better," he wrote. "They told me my results were great and that I could have my job forever if I wanted it, but I wasn't moving up, ever."

"Hero to Zero" never wrote again to tell us the next chapter of his story, but I would wager he's still a quant jock somewhere—unless his mind-set has radically changed.

Again, not everyone can be a leader or even wants to be. But if you're in the midst of a career-stall 10-10-10, it's worthwhile to ask yourself how you're perceived. If your company doesn't think you can manage, it may be managing you out.

STUCK ON THE OLD YOU

And then there's the career stall that occurs because we've got a reputation, earned or not, that we can't shake. Maybe we royally screwed up an assignment a few years back, or we were involved with a project or product that failed, or we were hired by a manager who later left the company under a cloud of controversy. In such cases, we're tainted by a prior activity or association.

But sometimes our embedded reputation has to do with something less concrete: limited expectations.

The daughter of a trucker and a restaurant manager, Jody was the first person in her family to attend college, and she still counts her graduation day from the state university as the proudest of her life. With a degree in accounting and a 3.5 GPA, she soon landed a job as a bookkeeper with a machine manufacturer in Ohio.

For five years, Jody flawlessly executed her responsibilities, and according to her manager, brought energy, insight, and creative solutions to the job. Her colleagues liked her too; she was considered a team player who valued honesty and hard work.

No wonder Jody was perplexed when she didn't receive the small promotion she applied for in her division. She sought out her boss and asked why. "I know I can do the job," she insisted.

"I know that too," her boss agreed. "But that position is for an MBA."

Undeterred, Jody went back to work with increased determination—and earned her MBA on the side. Eighteen months later, degree in hand, she applied for a promotion again—and again was turned down. She was devastated.

"I don't understand," she confronted her manager. "I got the credential you wanted."

Her boss had no good answer—at least, not an answer she could admit. But I've seen cases like Jody's enough times to know that Jody was the "victim" of her embedded reputation. In her company's mind, she would always be a bookkeeper, MBA or not.

In time, Jody put her advanced degree to good use at another company, which was able to see her credentials, skills, and potential with fresh eyes.

And that's a happy ending to remember if you find yourself in a career dilemma where probing with 10-10-10 leads to the realization that you're stalled because you've changed, but your reputation has not.

THE WORK-LIFE MYTH

A final source of career angst—and perhaps the most emotional one—is work-life balance. Think about Lynne Scott Jackson, whose dreams of a new business were just coming to fruition when her elderly parents suddenly demanded her attention. Or recall Jackie Majors, the high-flying corporate executive who was spurred to use 10-10-10 by her young daughter's remoteness. 10-10-10 opened both women to the consequences of their options across three time frames, and helped them discover solutions that met their deepest wants and needs.

Those wants and needs, incidentally, were quite different. Lynne wanted more work in her work-life balance equation. Jackie, less.

My point? That you cannot 10-10-10 a work-life dilemma without being very clear with yourself about the relative importance of your values. Because balance is a myth. When it comes to conflicts between your work and your personal time, you need to make trade-offs. That's why I prefer the term "work-life choices." If you value professional achievement and wealth, you are de facto *choosing* that the amount of time you devote to work will be more than the amount of time you devote to all other activities. If your top value is being there all the time for your kids while they grow up, you are de facto *choosing* not to be a CEO. Climbing the corporate ladder requires unimpeded availability and unfettered commitment. And so does being an ever-present mother.

You cannot have it all, all at the same time.

But if you think that point is obvious to everyone, or even widely accepted, you'd be surprised.

Time and again, I've encountered women who are struggling through a 10-10-10, thinking it has the magical ability to put their lives in perfect "balance," with a big job, great kids, a happy marriage, fun vacations, and toned thighs.

Invariably, I tell them something's gotta give. Eliminate two of those goals. Or be realistic—eliminate three. I offer my own case as evidence. In the years when building my career at *HBR* was a top priority, I missed school plays, ice skating performances, and plenty of nights of homework. Dinner was often hot dogs and apple slices. And my thighs were definitely not toned.

I was living by a set of values that I had chosen with my eyes open—and therefore I had to own the consequences.

Sure, I could have blamed my company for not being more family-friendly. But I knew business exists to make profits, not to make my life pleasant. I could have blamed society for not making men carry half the load of child-rearing. But why be angry at a system that is thousands of years old and predicated on the biological reality that women bear children?

I was a realist, I guess. I still am. That's why when it comes to career dilemmas around work-life "balance," I urge you not to just think hard about your values but to actually rank them. Only then will your 10-10-10 reflect the trade-offs you've chosen to live by.

WE'RE GOING TO DISNEYLAND

Not to sound harsh! I know all too well that those ten or fifteen years when you are trying to be all you can be at work and at home can feel like an unmitigated series of little agonies. I know you can have days and weeks on end where you feel as if your choices are making no one fully happy, especially you.

I know all too well also that working mothers spend

each day in a constant inner dialogue, endlessly making King Solomon–like choices. 10-10-10 can help, but even with its assistance, many work-life choices still carry their fair share of *weltschmerz*. I just want to be honest about that. 10-10-10 is the best parenting tool I know of; I've seen its power and effectiveness more times than I can count. But it won't *banish* your work-life conflicts; it will help you understand them, manage through them, and make peace with them.

Barbara, a West Coast retail executive, married in her twenties, but she and her husband, a neurologist, never found the time or inclination to have children as both of their careers expanded. But just after Barbara's forty-fifth birthday, a case of "baby fever" struck, as she puts it. "Both John and I suddenly realized something huge was missing from our lives. We had each other, but we desperately wanted a family. It was like we woke up."

After an unsuccessful year of trying to get pregnant, the couple decided to adopt an infant from China. They had no mixed feelings—"A child is a child, and every child is a blessing," as Barbara told me—but the process delayed their dreams of creating a family for another year. Finally, the couple flew to Beijing to pick up their new daughter, Amy.

On the flight back to the United States, however, Barbara began to feel nauseous. And she stayed nauseous for another three weeks after the family arrived home. It was morning sickness—and seven months later, another daughter was born. The couple named her Jesse and moved a second crib into Amy's room.

The years that followed were one continuous juggling act, as John and Barbara adjusted to dual career parenthood and the jolt of two children arriving within one year. Yes, they adored the girls; yes, they were happy. But they were constantly exhausted. John changed hospitals to work closer to home and switched to the more predictable schedule of the emergency room. Barbara learned the fine art of managing babysitters. And, in order to spend more time with her daughters in the morning, she started going into the office every Saturday night to do paperwork.

Finally, when the girls were five and six, Barbara and John decided they needed to feel normal for a change; they needed a vacation at Disneyland.

Ever the good corporate employee, Barbara gave her bosses six months' notice about the dates of her week off. Meanwhile, at home, she and John started to spend evenings with the girls in front of the computer, planning every minute of the trip. There would be breakfast with Tinkerbell, lunch with Cinderella, with rides on Space Mountain and It's a Small World in between.

Then, a week before their departure, Barbara's boss, a woman about her own age, sent her a curt email. The CEO was coming for a visit; Barbara's vacation had to wait.

Fighting waves of shock and anger, Barbara walked to her boss's office a few doors away. "I just can't cancel my trip," she said, trying to sound composed. "I promised the girls."

Her boss considered her coolly. "Do you think I got

where I am in this company without making sacrifices?" she asked. "Do you think just because you have young children you're exempt? Men have young children too, by the way."

The executive checked her BlackBerry and then returned her attention to Barbara. "My children are nineteen and twenty-four now," she said. "They're healthy, happy adults. And I worked fifty hours a week every year of their lives."

That evening at home, Barbara turned the problem over to 10-10-10. First she reviewed her values. Not only did she love her work, she was the major breadwinner for her family. But she had started motherhood so late in life, she told herself, that she couldn't take a moment of it for granted. More than anything, she wanted her girls to know her as an individual, not as a cyclone whipping through their lives. She wanted to know them too, not just when they were in trouble and she *had* to be there, but also in the unstructured moments.

In ten minutes, either decision left her with a crisis on her hands: a disappointed boss or a dejected pair of girls.

The ten-month picture was more nuanced. Barbara sensed her boss might back off from her hard-line stance. "She knew, underneath all that bluster, that I'd paid my dues along the way," Barbara told me. "I had some chits in the bank. I'd canceled many a vacation before. In fact, I probably had enough chits to go back to her and make a strong argument about my record of 'sacrifice.' She couldn't use one incident to define me."

On the other hand, Barbara reasoned, the ten-month

impact of a no-go decision would still be reverberating at home, as the girls continued to live with the fact that Mommy's work always came before them and that her promises were not to be trusted.

In ten years, Barbara calculated, she and John would be sixty-two, three years from retirement, and the girls would be teenagers. At that time, she asked herself, wouldn't trust and intimacy with her daughters be worth more than finishing her career one rung higher?

The family left for Disneyland as planned.

A week later, Barbara returned to work to find an email from her boss, reporting that the meeting with the CEO went very well, and suggesting ways she might immediately follow up with him on certain strategic initiatives.

"I admit, I felt a real pang when I saw her message. I thought, 'Oh no, I *did* screw up,'" Barbara told me. "But then I remembered how I had made my decision—with my eyes wide open. 10-10-10 was my little guilt eraser."

She made a note of her boss's request and got back to her life.

OLIVIA'S LAMENT

A few nights ago, I looked up from writing a column to see Sophia standing in front of my desk with a beautiful young woman. I must have looked confused, because Sophia burst into laughter. "Mom, come on—it's Olivia!" she cried.

Of course it was—all I needed to do was squint, and I could see the spunky little next-door neighbor I had once adored and hadn't seen for a few years. Now, it turned out, she was a college student in search of a major, and after an evening chatting with Sophia about her confusion, they'd decided to seek my advice.

"Oh, Mrs. Welch, it's making me crazy," Olivia started in. "I want a great career, something important and exciting—and not ditsy. I just don't know doing what."

I loved the "not ditsy" part, but that's not what struck me the most about Olivia's lament. It was the realization that she was experiencing her first career dilemma. I knew that if she was like the rest of us, many more would surely follow.

I told her so.

"Oh no," she immediately protested, "I want to be like you."

I was touched by her vote of confidence. But the truth is, I may have known what I wanted to be when I grew up long before I grew up, but when I finally did grow up, I still had moments of career confusion and even despair. I left Miami with my heart torn in two, one side pounding with grief over leaving the work I loved, and the other with excitement about the career I thought I might be able to build in Boston. As I stood in my driveway saying goodbye to my coworkers, my car packed with my every earthly belonging for the trip North, I remember taking a long, last inhale of the soft tropical air and wondering why I couldn't muster a little of Oriana's courage when I needed it most. I was still crying when I crossed the border into Georgia.

No matter what your career, I assured Olivia, you will have career dilemmas.

And you will resolve them. By understanding where they come from—and by understanding yourself.

CHAPTER SEVEN

Teach Your Children Well

10-10-10 as Your Partner in Parenting

One day when Marcus was five, apropos of nothing, he announced, "When I grow up, Mommy, I'm not going to tell you where I live." There wasn't an iota of malice in his words; I still remember the guileless smile on his face as he spoke, delighted as he was with his personal emancipation proclamation. But I still felt stung. I'd spent every day of Marcus's life pouring love into his adorable little vessel, only to discover in the most offhanded way that the payback might not be lifelong devotion.

"Oh no," I remember thinking, "this mommy thing is getting harder by the minute."

Oh no, indeed.

After twenty years on the job, I would submit that parenting is the most complex endeavor in the world. It can reduce you to putty; it can enrage or humiliate you. It can break your heart. It can suffuse you with feelings of intimacy, pride, and joy so profound you don't know what you did to deserve such a blessing.

I'm not sure parenting can ever be easy, but by introducing greater clarity, consistency, and calm, 10-10-10 can make it easier, releasing you from guilt and doubt and building trust in both directions, child in parent and back the other way. All in, 10-10-10 markedly decreases the days when parenting feels haphazard and overwhelming, and increases the moments when you feel, "I'm being the parent I want to be, and heavens to Betsy, it seems to be working."

And—here's the best part—10-10-10 can make family life a lot more fun. In fact, I hold 10-10-10 responsible for one of the best laughs I've ever had, which occurred when the adorable little vessel of Marcus had grown into a strapping young man of sixteen. We were walking home together from a swim practice one afternoon when he turned to me and, apropos of nothing, gave me a hug. "You know, Mom," he said, "when I get married, maybe you can move into my house and raise my kids. That would be good."

MOMMY IN THE MIDDLE

I started 10-10-10ing parental decisions soon after I returned from Hawaii, the hula skirt incident fresh in mind, and I haven't let up since. But one of my earliest applications of the process remains my favorite. One morning not long after I became a single mother, I promised the kids I would be home in time to make them dinner, and more important, to watch our favorite sitcom, *Malcolm in the Middle*. The kids loved that show because wily young Malcolm always ended up getting what he wanted in life, despite the interference of his screwy family. I loved it because Malcolm's mother had occasional bouts of so-called Level-Five Rage that her children managed to find endearing.

But at the office that evening as I was packing my briefcase, my boss caught up with me. "Bad news—the Carter piece just fell through," she said. "I need you to stay late."

I cringed. "How late?"

"A few more hours," she answered apologetically. "I'm sorry, but it's an emergency."

Now, my values as a mother were actually very clear to me at that point in my life. I firmly believed that my main responsibility was to teach my children the character trait of goodness—meaning compassion, honesty, and authenticity. I also believed that children benefited when their parents led happy, meaningful lives, which was why I needed to work full-time. My final value as a parent was shared respect. Some mothers might strive to be adored or obeyed. I wanted to build a family that could talk.

In ten minutes, staying at work would mean there would be talk all right. There would also likely be serious moaning and groaning, as in, "You promised, Mom!" and "Why does work always come first?" On the other hand, staying at work could only engender a positive response from my boss, as she noted my availability in her moment of need.

In ten months? Well, about that time, I knew I would be coming up for my performance appraisal, and I could be pretty certain my boss would still hold in her mind the memory of me hanging in there when it mattered. At home, my kids and I would be watching the continuing saga of *Malcolm,* my one MIA episode washed from their minds by my more typical conduct, which was a pretty solid record of being there and relatively rare bouts of Level-Five Rage.

In ten years, my decision was a moot point. Staying at work or leaving for home—one little choice about one little evening wouldn't matter either way in the big picture.

My dilemma suddenly became a no-brainer. The foreseeable future of my professional life trumped my kids' pressing desires, and would perhaps even remind them that the world did not revolve around their uninterrupted satisfaction, not a bad lesson from my perspective. I walked back to the office and told my boss I was in for the duration. "Thanks a million, Suzy" was her grateful reply.

Then I called home to report the news. The eruption was as predicted, but it was over in about five minutes; it ended right after I asked the babysitter to put me on speaker phone and I walked the kids through my 10-10-10 thinking. There was a moment of silence, then a chorus of little "Hmms" and "OKs." Sophia even promised to fill me in on the missed episode the next morning.

GETTING STRATEGIC

Soon after that incident, I started mentioning 10-10-10 to my working-mother friends, and they were among its earliest adopters. One used it to decide whether to heed her son's plea to quit an extracurricular science program, another to work through a conflict with her teenage daughter about summer plans. 10-10-10, I was told by these mothers and others like them, just made thorny parenting decisions simpler and more efficient.

Over time, I've come to realize that 10-10-10's immediate appeal as a parenting strategy is linked to its dependable capacity to backstop gut calls. Some parenting decisions give you time to ponder, but plenty don't. Can we take the car to the party? Can I sleep over at John's house tonight? Can I borrow twenty bucks to go to the mall with my friends? It's not like your kid ever asks you such questions with a week to spare, or in circumstances conducive to clearheaded thinking. These questions are typically posed on the fly, with an audience of friends in the room. Just as often, kids ask you to hurry up and make an important judgment call when you're distracted. My own children, for instance, have perfected the art of asking for permission when I'm on the phone, running late, or about to get in the car.

Fortunately, you can conduct a 10-10-10 analysis in the same amount of time it takes to hem and haw and finally give in. And you can deliver the reasoning behind your decision in the same amount of time as it takes to deliver your gut call with all its qualifiers and warnings attached. Remember Natalie, the mother who was trying to decide whether to attend her uncle's funeral? One son was pressuring her for a lift to soccer, the other needed a ride to the orthodontist, and every instinct was telling her to surrender to logistics. But in less than two minutes, she made a more sound decision. If she were to teach the values of responsibility and respect to her boys, she had to demonstrate them with her actions. She went to the service.

Just as with problems in love and at work, 10-10-10 also overrides our autopilot neurological biases and interrupts the closed-loop thinking that so often accompanies stressful parenting situations. That was the case with Paula, whose son was begging her to change schools. 10-10-10's methodology opened her mind to advice coming from an unlikely source—a taciturn math teacher. Ultimately, by impelling her to listen to someone she didn't like, 10-10-10 helped Paula get to the root of Hooper's real struggle.

THE G-WORD

But 10-10-10 transforms parenting decisions for another reason: it's an antidote to the cultural zeitgeist around motherhood—the white noise of opinions and directives that has an inescapable way of infusing doubt into our minds and guilt into our lives.

There, I said it, the G-word—guilt.

If you're a parent and you don't have a consistent operating principle like 10-10-10, guilt can be your constant companion.

That's in no small part because American society today is engaged in a contentious debate about the right way to raise children, with the main battle line drawn over whether mothers should stay at home or work, or some of both. The so-called Mommy Wars have spawned a cottage industry of books and articles, but they play out perhaps most widely among dueling mommy blogs, one of the most active communities on the web. From what I have observed, some mommy blogs are entirely neutral, serving as cyber coffee shops for the friendly exchange of parenting tips. But others are virulently politicized, creating a kind of electronic public square for mothers to lambaste each other about their respective work-life choices.

You don't have to go online, though, to step into the fray. I'll never forget the cocktail party I attended where a stay-at-home mother I'll call Lillian grew so annoyed with a story I was telling about my job that she abruptly cut me off with the salvo, "You working mothers think you're so important, it kills me."

"I don't think that!" I automatically shot back.

Lillian groaned in disgust. "Yes, you do," she said. "You think stay-at-home mothers like me just don't have the balls to get out there and cut it in the working world like you do."

Again I objected, but Lillian waved me off dismissively. "You go into your offices with your working-mommy friends and you laugh at us and say, 'What do they *do* all day?'" she asserted. "You think we're trivial. Don't you?"

My response was yet again denial—this was a cocktail party after all—but Lillian had me. My working-mother friends and I had on occasion cluck-clucked stay-at-home mothers. Some of my colleagues couldn't imagine how full-time mothers could stand the tedium of child care and household drudgery. Weren't they bored to death? Didn't they understand that they'd wake up to an empty house in twenty years, only to discover their kids had meaningful, rewarding futures—but they did not?

"Stay-at-home mothers *confuse* working mothers," I finally offered.

"You confuse yourself," she replied, "by not listening to what your guilt is telling you."

The G-word hung in the air between us for a moment before I made one last lame attempt at detente. "My sisters stay at home with their kids," I said, "and they feel guilty about *not* working about as often as I feel guilty *for* working."

"I doubt it" was Lillian's dry retort.

It was my turn to groan. There was, it seemed, no middle ground between us. We parted ways, and while I don't know Lillian's take on the conversation, I can tell you that it left me feeling just like every kind of mother today: defensive and not a little ambivalent.

A BLACK BELT IN TRUST

10-10-10 is your companion, and a very effective one too, in the never-ending quest to eradicate those feelings.

A year or two after my *Malcolm in the Middle* 10-10-10, work was continuing to plug along, but a possible promotion for me was looming. Because of that, my boss had suggested I grab every opportunity to show my commitment to the organization. I did, usually without any major impact on the home front. But then—a big break. I was asked to moderate a weekend offsite for the company.

Except . . . the offsite was scheduled for the exact day and time that Roscoe—twelve years old at the time—was going for his junior black belt. The test was a very serious affair, which would be held at the Uechi-Ryū karate headquarters in New Hampshire in front of a panel of sensei judges. It certainly stood to be the most important event in Roscoe's life to date. I knew this because every time Roscoe mentioned it to me, his cheeks flushed crimson and his voice got all wispy, like he might faint.

In ten minutes, I knew there was no easy way out. Agreeing to moderate the offsite was a huge boost for me professionally, and a huge loss for Roscoe, who would be hurt and confused. Hadn't I been telling him for years how much I admired the hard work and discipline he devoted to karate? Why did he have to be the only kid whose mother wasn't there to watch?

In ten months, I figured, it would be roughly the same zero-sum game. Yes, I could work harder than ever at work to make up for my absence at the offsite. Or I could fawn on Roscoe unrelentingly, attending every karate lesson and reiterating my admiration for its principles. But I couldn't fool myself: the consequences of either choice would still be reverberating.

Ten years out, though, there was a mind-clearing vision. I knew that, in the distant future, my career writ large would have reached the level where it belonged, a level not decided by one appearance at one offsite, but by a marathon of twists and turns along the way. Roscoe, however, would only get his black belt once. In ten years, he would be away at college. Our time until then could be precious or fraught. And I could not deny that it stood too big a chance of being the latter if I abandoned him at his first big moment of truth. He might never trust me to be there for him again.

That weekend as I watched Roscoe move through his precise *katas* one by one, not for a moment did I doubt I was in the right place.

Technically speaking of course, attending Roscoe's black belt exam was 180-degree turnaround from my previous *Malcolm in the Middle* 10-10-10 decision. My values hadn't changed. My assessment of their impact did. And nothing got in the way of my acting according to that insight—not gut, not guilt, not anxiety, and not the cultural static about what mothers should and shouldn't do.

RAISING CAIN

A few years ago, I was very intrigued to read *The Nurture Assumption: Why Children Turn Out the Way They Do* by developmental psychologist Judith Rich Harris. The provocative thesis of the book would give pause to any parent in today's environment, as it asserts that children are primarily formed by their genes and the values of their peer groups. Parents, Harris concludes, deserve neither credit nor blame for the way their children behave.

If only everyone agreed! Think of the huge exhale we would hear. But instead, our popular culture sends a radically different message: "Perfect parents produce perfect children; wayward parents reap what they sow." And so it is that, along with the *sturm und drang* over whether mothers should work outside the home, parents are also bombarded with an encyclopedia of advice about all the things they can do to raise successful progeny. Sign your kids up for the soccer team in the fall and Little League in the spring. Make sure they start piano lessons by age three. Buy them the high-end laptop. Put them in SAT tutoring in tenth grade. And don't forget the Chinese lessons.

On TV, Dr. Phil and Dr. Laura (not to mention a scad of lesser lights) scold parents on a daily basis. Every bookstore has aisles devoted to the topic of rearing kids the right way. And consider the magazine features devoted to Britney Spears's mothering skills or the reality shows that shine a spotlight on dysfunctional parenting styles. I myself will admit to an occasional evening with the series *Wife Swap,* which, despite its prurient name, is nothing of the sort. Rather, it's a moralistic cautionary, in which two families exchange mothers for a week, only to see mayhem erupt as disparate values collide.

The pressure to turn out super-children can afflict even resistant mothers who claim to place a high value on character. I confess! For years, I walked around saying I didn't care about my kids' grades and other credentials as long as they were "good human beings." But you should have seen me when Roscoe was competing in the national high school wrestling championships. I was cheering so hard for him to win, Jack practically had to revive me with smelling salts after every match. And when Roscoe ultimately lost in the sixth round, I literally had to lie down.

Afterward, a psychiatrist friend of mine gently helped

me understand my ghastly behavior. "Mothers these days compete with each other by keeping score with their children's successes," he said. "Given society's fixation on how to raise perfect children, it's nearly impossible not to."

He then urged me to call Roscoe and apologize for my sullen moping around when he decided to retire from wrestling in college. I definitely plan to get around to that very rational edict . . . someday.

A SEAT AT THE TABLE

As if the debate over child-rearing wasn't fraught enough, there's yet another complicating factor in the mix. The command-and-control model of parenting, where "father knows best" and everyone else shuts up, is long gone. Most kids today think they're adults by age fourteen or fifteen, and inasmuch, expect a seat at the decision-making table.

What's the source of this presumption? Surely it stems from the fact that modern kids know more about life at an earlier age than did children of generations past. How could they not? You can try to turn off the TV and outlaw the Internet in your house, but good luck banishing all forms of media unless you're living in a cult compound. I tried diligently to keep my home G-rated for years; I'm somewhat embarrassed to say I even banned *The Simpsons* for about a nanosecond because I feared it was too subversive. But I gave up the ghost in 1998 when Sophia, then nine years old, took one look at a photo of Monica Lewinsky in the newspaper and, with more insouciance than a mother might like, opined, "What's the big deal? It wasn't real sex."

I don't want to sound like a cranky old lady here, decrying the lost youth of "kids these days." I can see one perfectly legitimate reason why teenagers now believe they're grown-ups—so many of their role models are doing adult things. We live in an economy where Mary-Kate and Ashley Olsen, once sitcom starlets, were running a multimillion-dollar enterprise before they finished high school. Miley Cyrus, heroine of the adolescent set, and Lil' Bow Wow, the teen rapper, are staples of the music industry. If these young people have adult supervision, it's usually kept out of sight.

But in the real world, most adults do stay on the scene. And because that scene is more complex than ever before, 10-10-10 is that much more relevant, lowering the cacophony of commentary from experts, scolds, fellow parents, and your kids themselves by helping you make choices based upon your own deliberately selected parenting values. It provides a framework and a shared language to bring our children into the decision-making process without undermining their essential independence. In sum, 10-10-10 produces the kind of decisions that parents in this era need and kids want: grounded, consistent, and transparent.

MEAN GIRLS

Rick, a single father from Minneapolis, found himself in a painful parental dilemma when a rude wake-up call—

literally—alerted him to the fact that his fifteen-year-old daughter was spiraling away from him.

Tina played on the school soccer team and received decent grades, but her hobby, according to Rick, was "clique warfare." She would spend hours each night on the computer, gossiping on Instant Messenger and starting catfights with other girls. Rick hated the behavior but felt helpless to stop it. "I told myself that all teenage girls acted like Tina," he recalls. "I thought her meanness would stop."

It didn't, and a few weeks later, the mother of Briana, one of Tina's targets, called Rick and angrily demanded he do something. Rick was mortified, not just by the details of Tina's Facebook posts about Briana, which Briana's mother read to him, but by the fact that Tina seemed to be preying on Briana because she had a speech impediment.

"I was raising a daughter whose character was getting really ugly," Rick told me.

He turned to 10-10-10 to formulate a course of action, first surveying his options. He could punish Tina by taking away her computer access or he could send her to therapy to get at the root of her behavior, though he worried about the cost of the latter. Or he could concede to Tina's intermittent suggestions that she live with her mother, who, after a long struggle, was finally sober.

Next, Rick revisited his values. He regretted the emotional damage caused by his divorce and felt strongly that his children should be raised in the same household. Together, they had a family; apart, they had none. He also had a strong desire to teach his children his own midwestern values of humility and common sense.

Rick knew that he couldn't make his decision alone. Tina, like most teenagers, believed she had as much say in the particulars of her life as he did, if not more. He set aside an hour with Tina for a 10-10-10 conversation.

The talk lasted twice as long. When it got contentious—which it did more than a few times—Rick steered the discussion back to the 10-10-10 framework. If Tina, for instance, began to revisit old territory, Rick would redirect her by saying something like, "Let's look out at ten months." Finally, father and daughter settled on terms that they could both live with. Tina would remain with Rick and keep her computer access. They also decided it was worth it for Tina to enter therapy to work on her aggression toward Briana and other vulnerable girls. But before that even started, they agreed, Tina would write a note of apology to Briana and invite her over for dinner.

"Together we found the best solution for all three time frames," Rick reflected recently. "Because my focus was on getting Tina back on track so she would stop damaging people around her, I knew there had to be repercussions for her actions in the immediate term, as well as counseling for her underlying issues in the mid- and long term." He admitted that he was surprised and pleased by the insights Tina added to the conversation. For example, it was her idea to write Briana an apology, and she also suggested that perhaps her longtime association with another well-known "mean girl" should end. "There was no way Tina would have bought into any solution," Rick concluded, "if she hadn't been part of the process of reaching it."

BEYOND THE CALL OF DUTY

Rick's trauma with Tina was trying while it lasted and certainly gave Rick more than a few moments of bona fide, bone-chilling concern. But at its essence, it was the normal stuff of parenthood. Our kids step outside the lines; we nudge them back in. They step out again, we nudge a bit harder. Most days, raising our kids is simply a matter of making sure they live by the golden rule of Do Unto Others. They test; we correct.

Unfortunately, however, there are times when parenting goes far beyond the ordinary. Indeed, along the way, every parent faces a truly major crisis . . . or two or three. A teenage pregnancy. A drunk-driving arrest. Anorexia.

For Ana, a mother of three in the Detroit suburbs, the crisis was drugs.

Ana's son Bobby started smoking marijuana at thirteen. By seventeen, he had dropped out of school and was living with other drug users in a party house in the city, a move that sent shock waves through the tight-knit family. Ana's daughter, Kara, who was eleven at the time, lost her focus in school, and her eight-year-old son, Brian, withdrew into video games. Eventually, both kids dragged their mattresses into the basement to get away from the noise of their parents' nightly fights over Bobby's situation. Ana wanted to do everything to save her son; her husband, Gary, a metal worker in an automobile factory, wanted to disown Bobby and throw away the key.

For five years, Bobby came and went in his family's

house, staying only a few days at a time and invariably wreaking havoc. He stole money and sometimes punched Brian without provocation. The family continued its routine of school and work, but behind closed doors, nothing was normal. Bobby and Gary never spoke a word to each other, but their mutual hatred was palpable. Kara and Brian seemed to lead their lives in an invisible universe, coming and going on tiptoe. And yet, Ana repeatedly welcomed Bobby home, relieved to have him off the streets.

The situation finally came to a head when Bobby was twenty-three and Gary told Ana that if Bobby ever moved back in again, he would move out.

Ana's first reaction was fear. How would she support herself? What would happen to the kids? But soon anger rushed in too. Why was her husband making her choose between himself and their child?

In her turmoil, Ana was haunted by one question: What if Bobby died? She considered the piles of books stacked on her bedroom dresser, each full of advice on handling family members with addiction. One counseled her to have Bobby arrested for trespassing if he returned home, another argued that a mother should never "go negative" on a troubled child.

Ana needed to hear her own voice. Alone in her room one night, she turned to 10-10-10, and with it she discovered she had a powerful emerging value. She had to rescue Kara and Brian from the silent despair she had so long tried not to see. Her only choice was to draw them back closer to her, to give them hope for the future, and instill a sense that they had a mother who cared not just about her eldest son, but about them as well. It had been ages since she had attended one of Kara's softball games or asked Brian about his homework. And she couldn't even remember the last time she had asked either child to return to their old bedroom from their basement retreat.

Now, facing the question of whether she should allow Bobby to come home again, she considered her options—and their consequences—in ten minutes, ten months, and ten years.

In the first time frame, Ana reasoned, she simply couldn't let Gary walk out. His absence would destroy Kara and Brian, and undermine any chance of rebuilding the family they all so desperately needed to move forward.

In ten months, if she devoted herself to Kara and Brian and kept Bobby at bay, perhaps she and Gary could begin to reestablish their trust, and together they could start to create an environment in which their family could reinvent itself.

The ten-year picture was more painful for Ana, but she could no longer ignore it. Time and again, she had tried to rescue Bobby to no avail. Ultimately, she knew, he would live or die not because of her actions, but because of his own. The greatest gift she could give him—and her family—was a closed door.

That night, Ana told Gary of her decision to heed his wishes. In return, she asked him to join her in realizing her own dream of bringing Kara and Brian back into the fold.

When I checked in with Ana not long ago, she told me

Bobby had spent time in jail for drug possession and was currently working through a court-ordered rehabilitation program where she was able to visit him once a month. And yet, she sounded optimistic about her family's future, whether Bobby would be able to rejoin it or not. She mentioned Gary's plans to take Brian fishing over the summer break and Kara's improved grades.

But what excited her most was a change that had just occurred. Both children, she told me, had moved their mattresses back upstairs.

THE LONG HAUL OF LOVE

After I got off the phone with Ana, I had a real "There but for the grace of God go I" moment. Ana had clearly been a loving mother, yet her son had grown from a precocious toddler, to an errant teen, to a living nightmare. Yes, there were times—and plenty of them—when Ana felt gut-wrenching guilt over her decision to let her eldest son go. But she pushed through her doubt by revisiting the logic of her 10-10-10 thinking and dwelling in its good sense.

Although the details of every crisis differ, all parents with profoundly troubled or otherwise impaired children need a decision-making process to get them through months and even years of challenges, a process that will withstand the pressures of fear and instinct.

Connor was twelve when his mother, Maggie, began to notice that something about his behavior didn't seem right.

While Connor was often funny and endearing—he loved science fiction with a passion and showered love on the family's old dog—he often panicked over getting to the bus on time and he could become positively frantic about the tiniest disturbances of order around the house, such as how his sock drawer was arranged.

For weeks, Maggie watched Connor slip deeper and deeper into a well of anxiety. At last, desperate, she waited for him to leave for school one morning and looked for answers in his diary.

"I need to touch things," one entry began.

Maggie's heart stopped. "I realized I had passed my disease on to him," she told me. "And all I could think was, 'How could I do this? How could I have the hubris to think I could have children?' It was probably the saddest moment of my life."

Maggie's own battle with obsessive-compulsive disorder had started when she was a freshman in college. Two years later, she was also diagnosed with depression. Regardless, with herculean effort, she went on to build a successful career in advertising. And today she considers it one of her life's great victories that virtually no one knows of her daily battle with what author William Styron called "The Darkness Visible."

At the news of Connor's diagnosis, Maggie's impulse was to quit her job. Every day was becoming a logistical nightmare. She'd run to the office in the morning, then rush to pick Connor up at school for a doctor's appointment, bring him back to school, then run to her office again, and finally speed home to meet Connor and her older daughter at the bus. After dinner and homework, Maggie would collapse into bed, physically drained but with her mind racing about how she was going to make it through the next day's schedule.

"I have to stop the bleeding," Maggie announced to her husband Roy one night. "I need to be with Connor all the time."

But Roy wasn't so sure quitting made sense. Maybe, he suggested, a sense of guilt was making Maggie overreact to the situation. He urged Maggie to try 10-10-10, which she had previously used in dilemmas at work, and he volunteered to join her in the process as a sounding board.

Maggie agreed, but somehow, she still couldn't get past the first 10. She was so overwhelmed that stopping work seemed like the only option.

Roy pushed her, however, to imagine the ten-month scenario. Again, the answer felt obvious. "My instinct told me quitting would be great for Connor, *especially* in that time frame," Maggie said. "I could be all over his treatment. I could be all over him. Managing things, helping."

Maggie then moved on to the ten-year picture, with Roy urging her to take it slow and keep her emotions in check. Unexpectedly, that's when Maggie began to have second thoughts, not because she dreaded the long-term impact of quitting on her family and career, but because she couldn't predict it. "I realized I had no idea how Connor would be in ten years, or ten months for that matter," she told me. "A framework like 10-10-10 is only as good as the information you bring to it. And I didn't have all the data I needed."

To move forward, Maggie and Roy arranged a session with Connor's doctors and arrived equipped with a long list of questions about how Connor's condition was likely to unfold over time. It had taken Maggie decades to get her "cocktail" of medication for OCD and depression right. She knew psychopharmacology had become more precise, but feared the same prolonged process for her son.

The doctors, however, surprised Maggie with their optimism. In ten months, given twice-weekly behavioral therapy and medication, Connor would likely be much improved, they said, although his obsessions might never completely disappear. In two years, his disability would probably be invisible to all but his family and close friends. It was fine if Maggie wanted to be at home full-time, the doctors said, but it was not crucial, as long as she and her husband had some flexibility in their schedule to accompany him to occasional appointments.

"I had just expected to hear them tell me, 'Of course, you should be with your child every minute,'" Maggie recalls. "Instead, I realized it would be unhealthy for Connor to think his problem required a crisis response when what it really needed was just daily management, like asthma or diabetes or any other chronic disease."

Maggie's decision is now a year in the past. Connor, now a seventh grader at a large middle school, has good days and bad, with many more of the former. He's even gained enough self-confidence outside the house to take up swimming and join a chess club. "Connor's amazing. He gets how he's different. He's learning to live with it," she says. "We're all learning."

STRANDS OF HUMANITY

What an apt thought. Being a parent *is* about learning every day, never giving up on the challenge of loving and raising our children. Yes, it can be tempting to disengage emotionally from child-rearing, as the consequences of so many of our parenting decisions can take years to play out. And yes, today's cultural maelstrom, with all its conflicting messages, can often make parenting feel completely confounding. Especially when your children themselves step in and say, "I know enough about the world to make my own decisions, thank you."

One winter's evening when Roscoe was a sophomore at boarding school, he noticed that Justin, the awkward freshman who lived across the hall from him, was acting strange. He looked as if he was about to cry; he kept mentioning he was going to sleep early. Roscoe wanted to ignore what he saw. Wrestling practice had exhausted him and he had piles of homework to do.

Still, something was . . . off.

"What's wrong with you?" Roscoe suddenly found himself asking Justin. "Whatever—come to my room, OK? Let's talk."

Years later, Justin described what happened that night in an essay which he read to the school and also shared with me.

"I started crying. I told Roscoe everything. I told him what I was planning to do, about the pills I'd stockpiled. I'm sure he was uncomfortable, but he didn't show it," he wrote. "He told me about how he cried sometimes his freshman year. He told me how he had felt lonely and slightly geeky too. And then Roscoe sat next to me and hugged me with his hand on my head and asked me to be happy, because he would always stick up for me. I noticed our friendship for the first time, the string connecting Roscoe and me, and then I saw them all, all the connections I had linking me to others.

"I realized that I couldn't cut all the strings from me without cutting someone else. My loneliness was tethered back by so many strands of humanity."

Sometimes our children teach us how to make decisions.

More often, however, it is our job in this noisy, complicated world to teach them how to live, so that they can come to see that each decision is a tether to humanity.

10-10-10 is our partner in that most precious duty.

CHAPTER EIGHT

Lean on Me

Friendship Lost and Found with 10-10-10

Sue Jacobson and I met for the first time on a tennis court. She was Camp Clear Lake's "Director of Racquet Sports," a hilarious overstatement, given the humble reality of the place; I was to be her "aide." Any kind of hierarchical arrangement between us, however, lasted about five minutes. We just liked each other too much, and before our first week of friendship was out, we were inseparable. During the day, we'd entertain the campers by playing practical jokes on each other. At night, we'd set out in pursuit of Hyannis's greasiest onion rings, driving around for hours on end in Sue's dilapidated convertible, with Blondie and Lene Lovich at full blast.

It was during one such escapade that Sue and I accidentally rear-ended a gang of tough girls from the local high school. We jumped out of our car to apologize, but they weren't having it. They surrounded us. "What's your weird problem?" the leader of the pack demanded to know, leaning ominously into Sue's face. Then, this being Cape Cod in 1978, she and her friends laughed uproariously and drove away.

The bizarre humor of the incident wasn't lost on us, though, and Sue and I immediately adopted the gang leader's question as our personal refrain. "What's your weird problem?" Sue whispered to me as I walked off the stage right after receiving my college diploma. I had the exact same question for her after she received hers.

A few years after college, still close friends, Sue and I both landed in Boston, me at the Associated Press, and Sue as chief of staff for the governor's wife, Kitty Dukakis. The concordance of our careers was serendipitous, and, as ambitious young women working in essentially the same industry, we found more things than ever to talk about. But our friendship remained primarily about laughter, even after I got married and Sue found a serious boyfriend in Michael, a surgical resident at a Boston hospital. Many weekends, we'd still steal away for a drive in Sue's car or a quick run for onion rings at the Howard Johnson's in Kenmore Square.

Then one day in 1984, Sue called me at home. "I can't be your friend anymore," she whispered and hung up. Did I think it was a joke at first? The answer is no. Sue's voice was so different and strange that I knew in the pit of my stomach that she was dead serious.

I had other friends, of course, and I filled the huge hole Sue left with more still, but I never stopped missing her, even after I met Jack, who became the dearest friend of my life. It only made me sad that Jack hadn't known Sue, and when I mentioned that, he would always frown. "There's a reason she went away," he would say. "You just don't know it yet."

A FRAGILE NECESSITY

Sue's inexplicable departure from my life was such a blow—a devastation, to be totally candid—that I told myself for years afterward that I would never trust her again, even if she came crawling back to me on hands and knees.

10-10-10 changed that. In time, it empowered me to open my heart to Sue again, and led both of us to understand why we had had to break apart in the first place.

Indeed, 10-10-10 can rescue all kinds of friendships. It can give one or both friends a framework for putting a struggling relationship into perspective, and lay out a road map for reviving it. It can clarify values—both those that are shared and those that may be pulling a friendship asunder. It can uncover assumptions and hidden expectations, which, unvoiced, can bring a friendship to the brink. And in a crisis, it can help paint a vivid picture of what it would take to save a friendship and what it would cost to lose it.

10-10-10 allows you to decide what kind of friends you need, and what kind of friend you want to be.

Because friendship comes in so many varieties, doesn't it? We have friends who have become dear to us because our paths cross so often that something simpatico has blossomed. Tanya Ntapalis has been cutting my hair forever. In terms of background, interests, and lifestyle, we have almost nothing in common, but we've shared every little bit of our personal histories along the way, from first dates to divorces. Last year, I attended the wake of Tanya's beloved Gram. I'd never met the departed, I told the fellow behind me when he asked, "but her granddaughter is a very good friend of mine."

And then there are memory friends, the people with whom we've shared a seminal period of our past. My husband still hangs out with a gang of guys he played ball with fifty years ago. They talk plenty about politics and the Red Sox, but the old days are never far from the conversation.

If you've ever said, "She's a mommy friend," or "He's a work friend," you know what an identity friendship feels like. And how important they can be. I don't know how I would have survived the early days of child-rearing had it not been for the advice of my mommy clutch—I can still hear Maria telling me, "Just put pizza in the blender, Suzy. The baby will live." Nor will I ever forget how Kim prayed with me when I had run out of hope over Sophia's adolescent antics.

But the best friendships of all, I've found, are those that combine all of the above elements. Your paths cross often enough to keep you current, you have history to ground you, and you have some form of shared identity to sustain you. In this way, good friends can become our most enjoyable and easiest relationships. They don't carry the responsibility of marriage, the stress of extended family, or the angst of raising children.

Ironically, therein lies friendship's inherent fragility. We love and need our friends. We turn to them for solace in times of crisis and rely on their unvarnished advice. But they often take a backseat to the other relationships in our lives. We're not bound to them by blood like our relatives, by legal documentation and cultural expectations like our spouses, or by a paycheck like our coworkers. Friends, practically by definition, can wait.

And when things start to go wrong in a friendship, we can walk away and pretend nothing in our lives has really changed. We can stay in the same house, work at the same job, and go about our daily business without obvious upheaval.

Besides, of course, the upheaval in our hearts.

CONTINENTAL DRIFT

Jeremy met Lucille as he stepped off the elevator on his first day of work at a Las Vegas real estate development firm. New to the job and the city, he was a bundle of nerves. The buttoned-up woman behind the receptionist station only redoubled his anxiety. He politely introduced himself and asked to be directed to his desk.

"Weren't you supposed to be here yesterday?" the receptionist snapped.

Jeremy's stomach dive-bombed—but then the receptionist broke into a huge bolt of laughter. "Welcome, welcome, new guy!" she cried, coming around to pump Jeremy's hand warmly.

Jeremy came to love Lucille's whole earthy approach, as different as it was from his. At thirty-two, Jeremy had spent most of his life in Fort Lauderdale, living with his parents. At forty-four, Lucille was a self-described "spinster" from a large Armenian family in Brooklyn. But the pair shared a love of White House politics, gossiping each day about news out of Washington. Their rapport was so palpable that some colleagues suspected they were a romantic item, a rumor that became something of an office joke after Jeremy introduced his colleagues to his life partner, Dan.

Lucille and Jeremy's bond grew deeper when Jeremy supported Lucille through the end of a long and troubled affair with a married man. Afterward, Lucille would often spend weekends with Jeremy, Dan, and other friends, who affectionately nicknamed her "The Den Mother."

But even with Jeremy's companionship, Lucille was struggling in Las Vegas. She missed her family back East, and she felt that her job was vulnerable. As a member of the firm's support staff, she knew that if the city's economy started to cool off, she'd be among the first to be let go. And there was another question that kept popping into her mind. By spending all her time with Jeremy, was she "accidentally on purpose" keeping herself out of the dating scene?

"I basically had whiplash," Lucille recalls of that period. "Obviously, I was never going to have kids, but I still had a chance of getting married. But to get married, I would have to move away from a friend that made me about as happy as I'd ever been."

After a few years of ambivalence, Lucille decided to accept a higher-paying job closer to home, in Hartford, Connecticut. Jeremy and Dan threw her a beautiful going-away party, and Lucille cried openly during Jeremy's touching farewell toast, in which he referred to her as "a friend for now and always."

But in the months that followed her move, Lucille found she just couldn't bring herself to return any of Jeremy's calls or emails. She was afraid of missing him so much that she'd end up hating Hartford, where her new life was slowly warming up. Jeremy wrote her a few times, asking if something was wrong, but finally stopped trying.

Six months passed. Then on Christmas Eve, in church with her family in Brooklyn, Lucille found herself praying to hear Jeremy's voice again. She had so much to tell him about her new job, which was harder but more fun than she had expected; she wanted to get his feedback on a single man at work she liked and who seemed to like her. Overwhelmed by emotion, Lucille went home to her old bedroom, determined to analyze her friendship with Jeremy using the logic of 10-10-10. Could she devote herself to her new life, she wondered, and keep her old friendship too?

In ten minutes, Lucille reasoned, contacting Jeremy was sure to be awkward. She would have to explain and apologize. Would he even forgive her? And talking to him might open up emotional floodgates that would set back her acclimation to her new life. Could she afford that risk?

Lucille then tried to imagine her life in ten months. She was sure to be more settled in her new job. It was in her nature to make her own happiness; self-pity simply bored her. Wouldn't *that* Lucille—the future Lucille—have room for Jeremy in her life?

Finally, Lucille thought about the ten-year consequences of her decision, especially in light of her values. She had always put family and friends first. They were her pride and joy, her comfort and her clan. And Jeremy was among the most treasured of the lot. Why in the world would she let him go? To avoid a little short-term poutiness?

It was past midnight in New York, but still early enough to call Las Vegas. Lucille grabbed the phone and dialed Jeremy's number. "We cried for about a half hour," she told me. "It was just like old times, only sweeter."

Two years have passed since that reconciliation. Lucille and Jeremy now communicate often by email, with updates about their lives, and call each other on holidays and birthdays. Of course, without daily contact and common work challenges, their friendship has changed. It's based more on memories than office camaraderie, but they've brought it back to life.

More memories are sure to be made.

VALUES DRIFT

Jeremy and Lucille's friendship hit a rough patch because they moved apart, not an uncommon phenomenon in our mobile world. Just as often, though, friendships hit a rough patch because *values* have drifted apart. The beliefs, goals, and priorities that once brought two people together no longer match, and may even be at odds.

As college roommates in Vermont for four years, Isabelle's and Sarah's lives were so intertwined that some people on campus couldn't tell them apart. They shared clothes, wore their hair the same length, ate at the same table in the dining hall, and attended the same parties. Their only difference, really, was academic. Isabelle majored in studio art, Sarah in math.

After graduation, both women moved to New York City. Isabelle became a conceptual artist, supporting herself with part-time waitress jobs to pay the rent for the small apartment she shared with her boyfriend, a drummer. Sarah eventually became an equities analyst on Wall Street and married a trader. And yet, even with their lifestyles growing apart, a sense of history continued to bind the women. Once every two months or so, with Sarah as the organizer, the couples met for a night of dinner and drinks.

A few years in, however, Isabelle started to find ways to wriggle out of the get-togethers. The problem was Sarah's husband, Bertram. Isabelle considered him a smug control freak, and it bothered her that Sarah was absorbing his conservative political and social views.

The next time Sarah called about dinner, Isabelle waited until she knew Sarah was at work to leave a return message about being unavailable. When she hung up the phone, Isabelle later told me, she felt like "a liar and a skunk."

Isabelle had heard about 10-10-10 from me—we met through a mutual friend—and decided to apply it to her dilemma. She liked that the process could help her look at her friendship through a "values prism" to determine whether her values and Sarah's had diverged too far. She framed her question as, "Should I try to save my friendship with Sarah or let it go?"

Immediately, though, Isabelle hit a roadblock. If she and Sarah didn't share any values, could an authentic relationship exist in any time frame?

"Basically, we're connected by the experiences that made us the women we've become," she told me. "And we have a shared desire to stay lifelong friends. That's like a badge of honor to both of us. But is it enough?"

To explore the answer to that question, Isabelle asked Sarah out for a dinner, just the two of them. Probably sensing the topic, Sarah agreed reluctantly. And in fact, her concerns weren't unfounded. The conversation was painful, even with 10-10-10 as a road map.

In the immediate future, the women agreed, there was no getting around the ever-widening gap in their values. Isabelle admitted that she didn't like Bertram. Sarah blurted out that she thought Isabelle's boyfriend was a "slacker." Isabelle told Sarah that her high-paying job had made her insensitive to the struggles of the underprivileged. "My high-paying job allows me to give more to charity than you ever will," Sarah shot back.

The dinner might have ended right there had there not been a process to keep the friends at the table. They proceeded to the next step, which was a consideration of the ten-month picture. Letting the friendship go, the women conceded, would remove a source of ongoing discomfort from both of their lives. Isabelle confessed that she had lied in her phone message about dates. Sarah replied, "And you thought I didn't know?"

But then Sarah reminded Isabelle that they had a college reunion coming up. "Should we just ignore each other there?" she asked pointedly. "Like every other pair of old friends that couldn't keep it going? I thought we were stronger than that."

A long silence lingered between the women.

"Let's be real," Isabelle said at last. "In ten years, you'll be living in the suburbs driving a BMW, and I'll still be living in Astoria, scraping by."

Sarah could only nod. She and Bertram were already looking for a house in Westchester County.

"How about this? What if we hang in there for the next couple of years and see where it goes? I love you. I love what we've lived through together," Isabelle went on. "Maybe the fact that we can be friends, despite our differences, could be a source of real pride for us."

The idea gave Sarah the first flutter of hope she'd felt all evening. She too knew the relationship had an iffy long-term future, but losing it in the midterm felt premature to her.

By the end of the evening, the women had decided that they would work together to respectfully acknowledge that their sensibilities were no longer parallel. They could start to see each other once a year or so to renew the shared goal of maintaining an authentic bond. It would be a nice night out, they agreed—alone.

Since that decision, Isabelle reports, "What Sarah and I have now—it's such a relief. We don't have to tiptoe around each other. The air has cleared. We're both looking forward to making it work in a new way."

A BRIDGE TOO FAR

Even with new terms, however, not all friendships can be saved. There's been an injury of some kind: an unpaid loan, say, or one rude remark too many. I know two women who, after thirty years of friendship, stopped speaking when their sons became entangled in a legal dispute.

More often, though, friendships end because staying together would just hurt too much. At such a juncture, 10-10-10 can help to clarify the reasons for parting, alleviate guilt, and bring a needed sense of closure.

I first met with Angela, a social worker in Baltimore, because I'd heard she had a great 10-10-10 story about buying a house. And she did. In fact, her house 10-10-10 story was such a good example of the process that for our first two hours together, that's all we talked about. Angela described how, with her thirtieth birthday looming, she had decided that the time had come to move out of her parents' place. When two different realtors failed to find the house she was looking for, Angela's relatives kept telling her she needed to be guided in her real estate search by a midterm horizon, not a long-term one. But Angela wanted to buy a home she would live in forever.

"You know, a lot of women wait for their knight in shining armor," she told me. "I wanted to take care of myself. My dream was that no one but me was going to decide my life."

That comment was my first clue that Angela's 10-10-10 decision was not just about real estate.

It was also about real friendship.

In ninth grade, Angela had met Rebecca, and they'd bonded immediately. "We found comfort in each other," Angela reflected. "There was no explaining to do. We both had trouble fitting in, except with each other."

Each girl weighed more than 220 pounds.

Through high school, Angela and Rebecca grew into a two-person universe in which they shared all their time and an ever-darker worldview. "There have been studies of overweight friends that show how they identify with each other and reinforce one another into obesity," Angela said. "Rebecca and I were the perfect example." The young women decided to live at home after high school and attend the same community college. After graduation, both took jobs nearby.

Just after Angela turned twenty-five, her father's health took a turn for the worse. Her sister was married and couldn't be around all the time, and her elderly mother needed help. There was no other option. Angela took a leave of absence from work to assume the majority of caretaking for her father. But her weight made every chore difficult. She was almost physically unable to feed her dad, take him to doctor appointments, or put him to bed.

One morning, Angela had an epiphany: "People need me here," she thought. It was time to dedicate her life to losing weight and becoming healthy. She immediately called Rebecca. "I'm going to lose weight, this time for real. Are you in?" she asked.

Rebecca said she was, and that afternoon, the friends drove to a local Weight Watchers center. But it was soon clear that Rebecca's heart wasn't in the project. As Angela's weight started dropping and her resolve intensified, Rebecca grew angry, frequently challenging Angela with the assertion, "I don't know you anymore."

Bit by bit, over the course of eighteen months, Angela started to let go of old patterns. For years, she had spent every evening snacking in front of the TV at Rebecca's house. Now she started taking long runs through their neighborhood and lifting weights at a local gym. Her weight dropped to 200 pounds, then 180, then 160. At the same time, she decided to pursue a longtime fascination with Buddhism—she had been raised as a Catholic—and eventually joined a temple in the next town. Still, for the sake of their friendship, Angela continued to spend most of her time with Rebecca. They watched their favorite old shows and rented movies, but conversation was becoming increasingly difficult. Food and clothing became off-limit topics, and Rebecca forbade Angela from talking about her exercise routine.

In silence, Angela reveled in how her life was changing. She reached her goal weight—150 pounds—and ran a mini-marathon. With her new vitality, she was better able to help her father, whose health had also improved, and they started to take walks together in a city park they loved. Angela's emergent self-confidence spilled over into her job as well, and one day she asked her boss for a small promotion. To her delight, she got it on the spot.

Angela kept the news from Rebecca for weeks, anticipating a negative reaction, but even without knowing of the promotion, Rebecca's criticism of Angela continued to heighten. Then one day her phone calls stopped all together. "I knew Rebecca was trying to force my hand," Angela told me.

It was a decision that Angela had been dreading. In the immediate future, she knew, breaking things off with Rebecca would be a blessing and a curse. Gone would be the constant low-level antagonism, but so too would be the one true friend she'd ever had. There were many wonderful things about Rebecca she would miss—her witty sarcasm and the way she never judged Angela's family, in particular her emotionally remote mother.

In ten months, the picture wasn't much more promising. Angela worried about her ability to make new friends; she still thought of herself as the "fat girl" in the room. Without Rebecca, there might be months or years of nights and weekends alone.

But it was the more distant future that most captured Angela's imagination. "When I thought about the ten-year time frame, and I saw the life I was working so hard to create, I knew Rebecca wasn't going to be in it," Angela said. "She couldn't be; her whole set of values was too different from mine. She was right. I had changed."

The next evening, sitting in Rebecca's familiar kitchen, Angela urged her friend for the last time to join forces with her, but Rebecca instantly grew disgusted. "You're making me hate you," she warned. Not wanting to end their long friendship in acrimony, Angela quietly left the house.

In the aftermath of that parting, Angela endured some lonely times. There were moments when the comfort of

Rebecca's friendship and their old lifestyle beckoned. But a fragile bond had been broken, and there was no chance of repair.

Angela poured her energy back into house-hunting, and finally her journey came to an end. She found a small condo that needed some repair, but reinventing the place from the boards up appealed to her. Today, she has built an active life around her new home—a "sanctuary," as she calls it—and often entertains her nieces and nephews there.

"Thinking about Rebecca still makes me very sad sometimes," Angela told me recently. "But my life went on."

Of course it did. When a meaningful friendship dies, just as when a marriage ends, eventually we all pick ourselves up. We can be damaged. We are invariably changed. But if we can make some kind of sense of the past, it is in our nature to face the future again, believing we are stronger and wiser for what we have experienced.

STARTING OVER

I too tried to move forward when my friendship with Sue Jacobson ended. But instead of feeling stronger and wiser, I mainly felt confused.

Then one summer day in 2002, I received a letter. I recognized my old friend's handwriting on the envelope immediately and ripped it open. "Dear Suzy, I don't know if you will remember me, but if you do, I want you to know that I am sorry," the note read. "Please let me explain." At the end was an email address.

I rushed to my computer. "Well, well, well, what a surprise," I typed. I wanted to sound cool, invulnerable.

But Sue's reply was open and direct. She told me that she had married Michael, the surgical resident, and that they had had two children. Over the years, she said, she had watched my life through the media, often reading my articles in *HBR*. "I was always rooting for you," she wrote.

Five minutes later, we were on the phone.

"I'm going to tell you what happened," she began, "but you have to promise not to hate Michael."

I couldn't imagine what Sue was talking about. When I had known Michael—albeit briefly—he had been a very square, very mild-mannered guy.

"All right," I assured her.

"Because Michael is a great man and a great husband, and I don't want you hating him."

"I said OK—"

"But back when we were dating, our friendship scared him. I would jump whenever you said jump, and we spent all our time together, and we had all those inside jokes too, like—"

"Our friendship *scared* him?" I interrupted her to ask.

"Listen, he told me it was him or you, Suzy," she said. "And I chose him."

For a long time, I was silent. Then Sue asked, "Are you going to hang up?"

"No!" I cried. I wasn't angry—I was relieved. Of all the explanations I had imagined, Michael feeling threatened by me was not among them. Yet it made perfect sense. He had been trying to build a meaningful relationship with Sue—a sacred, authentic thing, the kind of "third force" I spoke of earlier in this book—and I was interfering.

"What a good husband Michael must be" was all I could think of to say.

I asked Sue if I could think about her proposal to rekindle our friendship. She said sure, I could take all the time I wanted, as long as I didn't take enough time to do something stupid, like not call her back. "I am assuming you still have a weird problem," she ventured.

"Not one as big as yours," I replied, laughing despite myself.

Over the next few days, I thought about Sue nonstop. My gut was all over the place. Even with her good explanation—she'd made a values-driven choice I truly respected—I didn't think I could trust her anymore. On the other hand, I loved her zany personality and her smarts about everything from politics to family relations. After eighteen years, the idea of having a beer together was completely thrilling.

I turned to 10-10-10.

In ten minutes, I knew that trying again promised daunting unknowns. We would have to catch up. We would have to heal. And perhaps hardest of all, we would need to learn to trust each other again. Yes, *each other*. Did I forget to mention that in our phone call, Sue asked, "Why didn't you ever try to call *me*?" It was a legitimate question. Perhaps our friendship could never get over an injury as deep as the one we had inflicted on it ourselves.

In ten months, though, the awkwardness might be fading. We might even find common ground once again.

And in ten years—well, imagine that, I thought. We would be in our fifties. Our kids would be grown and we'd have plenty of time to tool around in my red Jeep looking for greasy onion rings. Our summer haunts, it turned out, were an hour away from each other.

I had nothing to lose by reconnecting with Sue, I decided, and an inimitable friendship to regain.

Our reconciliation ended up being remarkably swift. We arranged a visit and then another and another. We laughed as easily as ever and still shared many of the same sensibilities, but we had a new bond too. We both had happy marriages and demanding children, and we both spent the better portion of our days trying to figure out how to balance them with our active careers.

Our reunion, to be sure, was made easier when our husbands hit it off swimmingly, as did our kids. But at the center of our renewed friendship, it's still just the two of us, helping each other live with joy, not to mention perspective. Not long ago, when my son, Roscoe, and Sue's daughter, Elizabeth, were both applying to college at the same time, we pinged emails back and forth probably twenty times a day. "The guidance counselor won't look me in the eye. He knows she's not getting in. We're screwed," Sue would write, to which I would respond, "*We* are screwed. Roscoe just got a B-plus in Chinese. These stupid colleges only take kids with all As. I hate them. They don't deserve my son." And Sue would swiftly click back to me, "Let's kill ourselves together tonight."

In person, we've had even more fun. Last winter, we took our kids—all six of them—Christmas shopping at the mall. At one point, I steered the entourage into a dress store. But Sue was on to me in an instant. "Oh no, you don't," she whispered. "Not again. You can't make me do it."

"Oh come on, Sue," I pleaded. "Just try this." I pulled a tight little beaded number off the rack.

"Stop it!" she cried, grabbing the dress out of my hand and hanging it back up. "For God's sake, what is your weird problem?"

I took a long look at Sue's sensible shoes, and made a face that she knew all too well.

"What is *your* weird problem?" I naturally replied.

ALONE OR TOGETHER

Ah, friendship. The great, fragile, voluntary necessity of our lives. Ralph Waldo Emerson was right. A good friend is a "masterpiece of nature," rare and wondrous. The songwriter Bill Withers, perhaps a poet of lesser distinction, was on to something too. We all do need somebody to lean on.

Some friendships of course find their natural ending, like that of Angela and Rebecca. Others hum along without a blip for decades, like Jack and his high school pals. But in most every life, there are meaningful friendships that hit a crossroads, and we must decide whether to go forward alone or together.

It is at those turning points that 10-10-10 helps us see how our friendship's underlying dynamics have shifted, and as important, whether those changed dynamics can, and should, be overcome.

As soon as I finish writing, I'm going to give Sue a call.

I have a question to ask her.

And I know she has the same one for me.

CHAPTER NINE

The Mistletoe Dart

Some Thoughts on 10-10-10 and the Circle of Life

There have been two times in my life when I've felt as if I've just fallen through a trapdoor, my eyes blurry, my heart in my throat, my whole everything suddenly tumbling into a vast unknown.

The first occurred fifteen years ago when, with my marriage long gone in all but pretense, I saw a little "+" sign on a pregnancy test stick, and the second more than a decade later, when my mother's surgeon called to say, "Suzy, I'm sorry, but something has gone very wrong."

Beginnings and endings are petrifying.

Sure, some people greet a baby's arrival with serene composure and face the loss of a loved one with sage equanimity. But for most of us, most of the time, the seminal experiences of birth and death can bring us to our knees, even literally. They can rob us of our equilibrium; they can fill us with fear and confusion.

And our decisions often show for it.

The day I found out I was pregnant with Eve, I made one of the most costly judgment calls of my life—to keep on keeping on, chirpily, as if nothing was the matter in my house. If my beautiful baby was going to be born into a "regular" family, I told myself in a private panic, I had no other choice.

For the next five years, we all paid the price of my stubborn decision to stay married, as our family painfully unwound in slow motion. Today, a lot older, somewhat wiser, and finally the authenticity adherent I should have always been, I know that 10-10-10 could have intervened on our behalf.

Because 10-10-10 surely has a special role to play at beginnings and endings, when our emotions are at their most attenuated and our reasoning at its most vulnerable. When a baby is born or a dear one dies, sometimes all we know for certain is that nothing will ever be the same again. At such times, 10-10-10 can guide us through to that new future—a future that we purposefully build.

TO HAVE OR HAVE NOT

The roller-coaster emotionality of having a baby can actually begin long before conception.

It can start, in fact, with the very decision to have one, a topic that has the power to surface (or at least aggravate) every suppressed issue in a relationship. How committed are we? What kind of life do we want? Which one of us will work and how much? What role will our families play in our lives? How much freedom does each of us want?

A few years ago, after speaking about 10-10-10 to a group of MBAs, I was approached by a woman in her late twenties named Pam, who was working as a manager at a computer company and earning her degree at night. Pam's bearing was serious and intense—crisp blue suit, hair in a tight bun—but her expression betrayed more than a little free-floating anxiety. She needed an answer, it seemed, and soon enough, I found out to what. "Should I have a baby now," she asked me urgently, "or wait until after I'm promoted in two years?"

Pam's voice dropped and, in whispers, she gave me a quick rundown of all the circumstances complicating her decision. Her husband, a partner in his family's Greek restaurant business, wanted a baby immediately and believed it was a mother's duty to stay home with the children. But Pam loved her job, dreamed of a high-powered career, and wasn't sure she wanted a baby, *ever.* "I wish we had discussed this before we got married, but we were too in love," Pam said. "Guess I just figured it would work itself out."

She exhaled in a way that made her desperation palpable. "What does 10-10-10 say?" she wanted to know.

I reminded her that every 10-10-10 process starts with a survey of our personal values.

"Well, I know *mine,*" she blurted out in response. "They're just not the same as Theo's—or his mother's. Or his father's. Or his sister's! I am not pumping out babies for ten years and then going to work behind some cash register."

And at that moment, Pam knew, as did I, that the baby debate in her household was a symptom of a larger problem.

We both knew too that her 10-10-10 decision was already made. She only needed the courage to live by it.

IT'S ALL IN THE TIMING

Obviously, many couples are in sync about their values. But even then, they can disagree about when to bring a baby into their lives.

Ajitha and Rohan, you might recall, were eager to have a second child once their marriage was restored by Ajitha's 10-10-10 decision. But another 10-10-10 analysis, conducted together, suggested that they needed to wait.

"In ten minutes, we both felt that a new baby would be like a symbol of our renewed strength," Ajitha told me. "That whole feeling really got us going, 'Let's just do it! Let's have a baby right away.'" When the couple looked at the ten-month and ten-year scenarios, however, their enthusiasm was tempered by their professional challenges and goals. "A baby in the next few years, frankly, would be very hard," Ajitha said. "Neither of us wants to sacrifice our career."

10-10-10, ultimately, has impelled the couple to come to terms with the fact that, at some point, one of them will have to bend if their daughter Laya is to have a sibling. They haven't decided which one of them that will be yet, or when, but 10-10-10 has kept the dialogue open and focused on their shared purpose: a welcome addition to their lives.

GOING IT ALONE

Sometimes a 10-10-10 decision not only helps us decide when to have a baby, but with whom.

Divorced twice and nearing forty, Jerri, a dental hygienist I've known for almost ten years, thought she was dating the perfect man. Nick was also divorced, with custody of his two teenage boys and a steady job in construction.

But after a year, the couple started bickering. At first, it was about little things like scheduling, but soon the fights started to extend into larger issues, like the boys' behavior.

Finally, the relationship came to a crossroads you might not expect. Nick asked Jerri to marry him. A solid commitment, he said, would solve their problems.

Excited and flustered, Jerri agreed.

Yet the quarreling continued.

One day Jerri asked me if I could 10-10-10 a question with her: Should she marry Nick right away or wait a year to give herself more time to plan the event?

We had barely made it through the consequences of the ten-minute scenario, though, when Jerri threw up her hands. "Forget it, we have to get married *now,*" she pronounced. "I can't wait any longer for a baby. I need to be a mother. I'm ready. It's all I want in life."

I pressed her to think of the ten-year implications of

that value. She looked surprised for a moment, then answered, "Not good."

Fiercely independent, Jerri had always been a person with a high need for "alone time," as she put it. Moreover, disappointed twice in marriage, Jerri basically didn't trust the institution or the commitment it demanded. "I want to be in charge of my own life, with no one owning me," she said as we continued our 10-10-10. "Nick has one picture of marriage and I have another. I can't bring a baby into that." The realization was especially poignant for Jerri, as she had been raised by parents who had warred incessantly.

With both sadness and relief, Jerri soon ended her relationship with Nick, and today is exploring options to become a single mother through adoption.

"No fancy dress and bouquet," she says, "but I think I'm on my way to my own version of a family—a family that could really work, because it's the family I know that I want."

THE EVIL HORMONE GENIE

I had been working as a management consultant at Bain & Company for six months when my boss Andy Wasynczuk called me into the conference room for a performance review. Along with being a great mentor, Andy was a great friend, and I knew before the meeting even began that he was generally happy with my work.

The first half of our conversation went as expected, but then Andy turned to the ways in which I could improve my performance. For instance, Andy suggested, it wasn't a particularly good use of my time to fixate on the aesthetic quality of my PowerPoint slides.

"What's it to you?" I muttered in response. "I'm not paid by the hour."

Stunned, Andy took my comment as a joke and moved on.

"Another thing to think about is your reliance on using regression analysis," he said. "There are other computer tools that work as well and are often more appropriate—"

"You have a *problem* with regression analysis?" I cut him off. "I find that very odd for a person trained as an engineer."

"I don't have a problem with regression, exactly," Andy replied patiently, but then, taking in my petulant expression, he stopped dead in his tracks. "Let's continue this conversation later," he said, sounding mystified. "You're definitely not in receive-mode today."

"Get used to it," I snarled. "This is the *new* me."

Well, it was the *pregnant* me. And while my mood did eventually right itself, my meeting with Andy was my first glimpse into the evil hormone genie that invades your body with conception.

That genie can become positively demented after the baby is born too, especially after it bumps into its best friend and soul mate, exhaustion.

Now, I'm not talking about anything clinical here, like the kind of severe postpartum depression that can lay some new mothers low. Such situations most certainly require professional counseling or pharmaceutical intervention.

No, I'm talking about standard-issue new-baby madness. The kind that makes you say hurtful things to people who care about you and forces you to make decisions as if there is no tomorrow. The kind of baby madness that operates from the assumption that there is only right now, this minute, and you are tired and fat and the house is a mess and no one is helping you and the baby isn't pooping right. And you are tired and fat—*very* tired and *very* fat.

That kind of madness.

AND BABY MAKES THREE

Bethany had wanted a baby for as long as she could remember, and she spent her pregnancy in a state of blissful expectation, readying the bassinet, preparing homemade organic baby food, and picking out adorable announcements. She and her husband Juan were especially excited about having their birth experience at home with the help of a midwife, avoiding all medical intervention.

But the couple was to learn the first lesson of parenthood when Bethany went into irregular labor three weeks before her due date: Babies have their own plans. Santiago was delivered by an emergency Cesarean section.

Once she was home from the hospital, Bethany found that nothing continued to go as she'd planned. She couldn't get Santi to latch on during breastfeeding and had to resort to bottles. Nor did Santi "find a schedule" as Bethany's baby books had said he would. At six weeks, he slept all day and wanted to play all night. And then, when Bethany thought she couldn't feel any more exhausted, Santi got a head cold that required medicine dispensed with an eyedropper every two hours, around the clock.

Bethany called Juan at work to report what was happening. "I need you to come home and let me sleep," she said. "I'm begging you, so I can stay up with him all night."

Juan was silent for a long minute. "I guess this means you aren't coming with me," he answered quietly. "Remember, this weekend? It's Julia and Greg's wedding."

Bethany slammed down the phone, practically shaking from fury. Of course she remembered the damn wedding. Julia was *her* cousin after all. But given the circumstances, she had just assumed Juan wouldn't go.

She grabbed her cell phone and typed Juan a text message: "I will never forgive you" is all it said.

Bethany was still in a rage when her mother came by later in the day to drop off groceries. While she was sympathetic to her daughter—Bethany had never looked more bedraggled—her mother urged her to 10-10-10 the situation. They formulated the question as, "Should Juan attend the wedding?" and got started.

In ten minutes, handling Santi alone during the weekend struck Bethany as a burden too heavy to bear. Her mother offered to help, but as Bethany told her, "You cannot be here twenty-four hours a day. Papa needs you."

But Bethany's mother urged her daughter to imagine the weekend without Juan, regardless. Wasn't there any scenario that made his absence tolerable?

"No," Bethany stated flatly, rolling her eyes. "None."

In ten months, her mother asked next, "What will it be like around here if Juan stays home this weekend?"

Bethany caught the drift of her mother's question immediately. As husbands went, Juan didn't demand much. He'd been a great help with Santi, forsaking all of his after-work activities, including going to the gym, his favorite way to unwind. If Bethany demanded he miss the wedding as well, his resentment might linger indefinitely. By contrast, if he went to the wedding, he might find renewed energy to help Bethany in the coming weeks and months.

Bethany and her mother turned to the ten-year picture. "That's too far off to matter," Bethany dismissed the notion. "Santi will be going to school. We'll have other kids. I'll be sleeping again. Everything will be normal."

All at once, she laughed at her accidental eureka. "And this crisis will be a distant memory," she said. "I must be making it into something so big because I'm so worn out."

An idea occurred to her just as the phone rang. It was Juan, calling to plead his case again. "I have a better idea," Bethany replied, surprising him with her sudden brightness. "Why don't we go with you? Everyone wants to meet Santi, and God knows he can stay up all night dancing with us."

Just hearing the plan out loud thrilled Bethany. "Santi is managing us," she told Juan. "We have to manage him. We have to bring him into our life, instead of the other way around."

"I love it," Juan cried.

In her changed physical and emotional state, Bethany had been living in the moment, every moment. But with

10-10-10's help, she began to see how things could change if she took it upon herself to forge the shape and feel of those moments, for the days, months, and years ahead.

FROM SNARKY TO SUBLIME

Maybe I sound like I have amnesia. My oldest child is twenty now, the youngest fourteen. It could be that I've forgotten how hard caring for a new life makes it to think about creating a deliberate one for yourself.

Or maybe I've just earned my perspective.

When Sophia was a baby, she was so easygoing that we called her our little Buddha. She never fussed, she never cried. She slept through the night when she was two weeks old. When she was done nursing, she used to look up at me with a dreamy smile, as if to say, "Nice going, Ma."

But she made up for lost time as a teenager. Of course she did. Once, at age fifteen, she was so errant—she has forbidden me from sharing the specifics—that I sat on the living room sofa for two hours and cried nonstop. Big, heaving stuff too. It wasn't the last time. By seventeen, though, she was back to being the Buddha again, a poised and thoughtful student, a constant friend, a mature and loving daughter.

Eve was the surliest baby you've ever seen—so grouchy, tough, and snappish it was as if the word "snarky" was invented for her. Even Abby, the sweetest dog in the world, couldn't take her constant pestering. In her only moment of canine misbehavior ever, she bit Eve on the face. At the emergency room, as we awaited stitches, a nurse asked if the dog was a problem.

"No," I told her, "the baby is."

But at Eve's last parent-teacher conference, I was informed that "Eve fills every room with light. She's kind and friendly to everyone. She's pure goodness."

"If you only knew her when," I thought to myself.

My friend Marybeth Turner used to fret that her daughter Caroline was sweet but very ordinary. "I'm afraid Ryan got all the talent and brains," she used to say, referring to her older son. "Caroline just sort of floats along in life. I worry about her."

A few years ago, Marybeth put Ryan and Caroline into tennis lessons—Ryan because he showed athletic promise, Caroline because she had nothing going on after school on Thursdays.

One day, waiting in the parking lot for the lessons to end, Marybeth looked up from her magazine to see the tennis teacher frantically tapping on her car window. "Are you Caroline's mother?" he asked. "We've been waiting for you to come in."

"Is there a problem?" Marybeth replied, her heart sinking. "Is Caroline being moved down to beginners?"

The teacher looked aghast. "Have you ever *seen* your daughter play tennis?" he cried.

Today, Caroline is ranked the sixtieth-best tennis player in the United States in the under-twelve category.

Babies have their own plans for you.

But because it's only natural not to think so, 10-10-10 is there to help.

DARKNESS FALLS

One spring day last year, I was driving Roscoe to an eye doctor appointment north of Boston—I will never forget how we were both belting out a Coldplay song along with the radio—when my cell phone rang. It was Jack, and he was weeping. A close friend, far too young and full of life, had died of a heart attack.

At the next exit, we swung around and sped home. I was running up the stairs to find Jack when my assistant intercepted me. "I have very bad news, Suzy," she said softly. Her expression was grave.

"I've already heard," I cried. "Jack called—"

She grabbed my hand. "This isn't about Tim. It's about Valerie," she said. The mention of my old friend's name stopped me in my tracks.

"What?"

"There's been a terrible car accident. Valerie was driving and—I'm sorry, I'm sorry—they're not sure she's going to make it."

The news was too much. "She'll make it," I asserted automatically. "She's my age—and my God, she's strong."

Tragically, Valerie wasn't strong enough.

For the months after that terrible day, our house was filled with the stages of bereavement that, sadly, many of us know too well—shock, denial, anger, bargaining, and finally acceptance. Although the truth is, I still cannot drive by Valerie's house without feeling awash in a wave of disbelief. Her garden is still there—why isn't she?

Death—unfair, unwanted, and so often unexpected—rarely gives us good answers. That is why when it steals away someone we love, we need our family and our friends to help us sort through the confusion in our hearts. And we need a framework for moving forward.

Alice and James met in New York in the late 1980s, she a struggling musician, he a struggling artist. They never expected to get married—James had a severe case anxiety that took much of his energy—but when Alice found herself pregnant, they took the subway to City Hall and exchanged tinfoil rings. Soon after, Hugo was born, and two years later, a second son, Leo, arrived. Alice took a job teaching music to keep the family afloat while James devoted himself full-time to sculpting.

A shotgun wedding and financial hardship aren't usually harbingers of a happy marriage, but they were for Alice and James. They scraped together enough money to buy a dilapidated loft in the Meatpacking District and delighted in making it their own, fashioning bolts of cheap gauzy fabric into a tent for the boys' bedroom. Alice grew to love her job and began to give private guitar lessons on weekends, taking enormous pride in her role as breadwinner. "I believed the world would someday discover James's talent," she told me.

She was right. After a decade of obscurity, James was signed on by a respected gallery and his work began to sell steadily. Alice quit her job and the family, with the boys then ten and twelve, moved to Greenwich Village. Even with their improved circumstances, however, James's anxiety remained, and his success seemed to exacerbate it. As the pressure to produce more pieces heightened, he started to medicate himself with a mixture of prescription drugs and alcohol.

He died of an overdose one day while Alice was at the supermarket.

For weeks after James's death, Alice felt like she was sleepwalking. She took the boys to school in the morning, watched TV all day, prepared dinner, and made sure the entire family was in bed by nine. "I was filled with rage, I think," Alice recalls, "but I blocked everything just to get by day to day. I had to stay centered for the boys."

About six months after James died, Alice lifted her eyes enough to look at the couple's bank account. The balance shocked her—there was barely enough left to make mortgage payments for the rest of the year.

"What do I do?" Alice found herself asking as she stood outside the bank, the winter's first snow coating her shoulders. She imagined running away to Jamaica, leaving her sons in her sister's care, or maybe taking the boys with her so they could all start over from scratch. Both plans were crazy, she knew, but what plan made sense? Alone in the cold, Alice dropped to her knees on the sidewalk and started to cry.

An elderly woman walking by rushed to her side. "Are you all right?" she exclaimed, lifting Alice by the elbow. "Should I get an ambulance?"

"I need my sister," Alice finally managed to say, and, handing her phone to the woman, hit speed dial to place the call.

The next morning, Alice and her sons sat in their living room, and with Alice's older sister as a facilitator, considered their future with 10-10-10. Their question: Where do we go from here?

In ten minutes, no one in the family could abide the thought of upheaval. The boys didn't want to leave their friends at school or the home they had known with their father. And Alice insisted that her current emotional state made moving or working impossible.

Softly, Alice's sister injected a dose of reality. The family's financial situation, she said, was precarious.

"How can we stay in our apartment and at our school?" one of the boys wanted to know. Alice wracked her mind for answers. "I could try to sell the sculptures Dad was working on when he died," she said, surprising herself with the idea. "Or we could look for a smaller place to live."

For the next half hour, the family bounced ideas off each other, and for the first time since James died, Alice felt present—in the room and in the moment.

When the conversation started to slow, Alice's sister raised the ten-year scenario. What kind of life, she asked, would the family want then?

Both boys spoke at once. They had already agreed between themselves that they would attend the same college somewhere—maybe in Boston, maybe on the West Coast—and they hoped to backpack through Europe one summer.

As they chatted away, Alice saw something new. Her boys were growing up and moving on. That wasn't wrong. It was inevitable; it was necessary.

But what did that mean for her own life?

She would need to become self-sufficient, Alice knew; that much was obvious. She needed a job. A career.

She had her decision. "It's not a question of if we should change our life," she told her sons. "We have to."

Over the next year, Alice sold some of James's art to shore up the family's finances and returned to her old teaching position. But she was most excited about a new "side" job, consulting to an online music service, a start-up venture.

Just after the first anniversary of James's memorial service, the family sold its apartment and moved to smaller quarters back in the Meatpacking District. The proceeds of the sale, Alice told the boys, would pay for their education for many years to come.

Of course, every loss like Alice's reverberates for years. Even with the help of 10-10-10, Alice and her sons experienced untold hours of sadness and struggle. But Alice no longer allows herself to dwell only on the challenges of the present and the unknowns of the distant future. She keeps her sights on the near horizon, a place where grace and hope seem to mingle.

REGRETTING REGRET

After my friend Valerie's funeral, I was touched by the number of people who came up to thank me for my eulogy. But what most of them really wanted to say, I discovered, was how sorry they were for never telling Valerie how much they loved her while they still had the chance.

One of the hardest parts of living within the specter of death is processing our own feelings of regret.

Jack and I were in Europe on business when my mother's surgeon tracked us down. His call was unexpected to put it mildly; knee replacements are usually pretty straightforward.

My mother had come out of the operation with flying colors. She had chatted with my father and eaten a small meal. But sometime during the night, a blood clot had left her knee and traveled to her brain.

After the surgeon called us with the news, my sister Della took the phone. "Suzy, I'm putting the receiver up to Mom's ear," she wept. "I think she can hear you. I think you . . . may need to say your goodbyes."

With Jack holding me tight, I too wept. "Mama, I love you, I love you," I said, "and I am so sorry for not thanking you more for everything—for everything you did for me. I never thanked you enough."

When Jack and I arrived at the hospital the next morning, my mother was still hanging on. Curled in her bed, overwhelmed by machinery, eyes fastened shut, she already looked gone. My father sat in a chair in the corner, stunned and motionless.

Our vigil was to last three weeks. My mother came and went, and when she came, she was so vague that my siblings and I could only hold her hand to comfort her. She was unreachable.

There were no decisions to be made in that terrible time. The decision would be made for us.

My mother was a fighter.

She still is.

Today, at eighty, she's back playing tennis. "My knees make me superwoman," she likes to say.

Her knees, and what they almost wrought, taught me about all the decisions I should have made, and didn't, as a daughter. They taught me about all the times I should have factored the irrevocable pain of loss—and the agony of regret—into my thinking. When I use 10-10-10, I think of those things now, when I need to. When decisions involve letting go. When they involve estrangement and forgiveness. 10-10-10, one moment at a time, helps us prevent regret. I know now how hard saying goodbye can be if you live and make your choices as if goodbye will never come.

Thank you, Mom, also for that.

FROM MY BOW

One summer's day when my children were young, I took them to the beach with my older sister Elin and my friend Lori. At the time, Elin's children were already teenagers off doing other things, and Lori was pregnant for the first time. So understandably, the two women could plop themselves down on a blanket to chat and read in the sunshine as if they hadn't a care in the world. Meanwhile, I stood by the shoreline having a heart attack as I watched four little bodies frolic in the choppy surf. "Someone's going to die," I kept thinking. "Right here on my watch, one of my kids is going to be washed out to sea, and then I might as well go in after them, and allow myself to be sucked up by the undertow and die too."

An hour later, when at last I had managed to coax my kids back to the blanket for lunch, I slumped down in a heap to recover for a few minutes.

"What's the matter?" Lori asked. By the sweet tone of her voice, I could tell she was oblivious about the hours of happy torment that awaited her.

"Suzy gets a little nutty when she thinks her children are going to drown," my sister reported.

"Have you no memory?" I snapped.

"I remember it all too well." Elin laughed. "But don't worry. You'll be reading magazines at the beach before you know it."

"I won't know how," I informed her. "I haven't had time to read a book in four years."

Suddenly Lori brightened. "Read poetry," she suggested. "Just as much pleasure in a fraction of the time. I'll send you a few books."

It is to Lori's great credit that she actually did so, and it is thanks to her encouragement that poetry did come to carry and comfort me through the next several years, as my children learned to swim, in more ways than one.

Somewhere in that period, I came upon Marilyn Nelson's poem "Mama's Promise." Lori was right. In the moments it took to read its scant sixty-three lines, I finally knew I was not alone in feeling the bittersweet irony of parenthood: that by giving our children life, we also give them danger, heartbreak, and loss.

"From my hands the poisoned apple," Nelson writes, *"from my bow the mistletoe dart."*

Were it not so. And yet beginnings and endings are part of the human condition. They *are* the human condition.

We are all living; we are all dying. In between, we have the gift of deciding how.

CONCLUSION

The Happiness List

Three years ago, Jack and I attended a beautiful New Year's Eve party. The host's home was decorated with dozens of twinkling lanterns, waiters swished around topping off glasses, and a jazz band filled the air with sparkly music. Around 10 PM, a bell tinkled for dinner, and we were swept into a grand tent lit by candelabra and festooned with flowers. If there was ever a moment to think "Ain't life grand?" it had arrived.

But then a strange thing happened. As soon as we sat down with our friends—there were eight of us at our table—instead of the oohing and aahing you might expect, one couple shushed us.

"It's crazy, I'm telling you. We've been trying to make a list since last week," exclaimed the wife. "And we can't come up with a dozen people who are really happy." She grabbed a piece of notebook paper out of her shiny evening purse and held it up for all of us to see. It was indeed a list of names, all but two or three scribbled out. "We've been dying to see you guys tonight because we can't believe this," her husband added to explain. "Can any of you name a dozen people who qualify?"

"As *happy*?" Jack asked, incredulous.

"Yes—just that," the wife replied, shaking her head as if she couldn't believe the answer herself. "I dare you. Name twelve people who are actually living the life they want. Come on."

At her invitation, each couple around the table entered into a sidebar conference. Jack's and my list came quickly, but just as quickly, we crossed names off it for one reason or another. Then, just as we were closing in on our quota, a man at the table cleared his throat to get everyone's attention.

"Well, people, I know this will come as a shock to you, but please scratch me off your lists," he said. "I'm not happy. I can't be. I'm Irish." We burst into laughter, but no one disagreed. The speaker was a wonderful person—funny, smart, and dear—but a true cranky-pants, committed to the Hobbesian notion that life is nasty, brutish, and short.

"I'm occasionally happy," his wife offered next, "but I won't be *fully* happy until the kids are settled." She paused as we all nodded empathetically. "And I'm not stressed out about my job. And I've lost fifteen pounds."

The two other couples at the table threw out a few names for consideration, but most were dismissed.

"Too bitter."

"Hates his wife."

"Living the picture."

"Jack's happy," I finally volunteered, to general concurrence. "Yes, he was on our list," the first wife said, waving her little piece of paper.

"And I am," I added meekly, getting the sense that maybe I hadn't made the cut.

Apparently I had. "You're a little intense," the wife said, "but a lot less than you used to be."

In the middle of all this, the soup was served, but none of us seemed to notice. We were engrossed—stymied—by the task of compiling our happiness lists.

Most of us were able to summon up a name or two; one friend volunteered a yoga teacher she knew who lived with her funky artist-husband in a converted barn on her parents' estate north of Boston. But others harrumphed at the choice. Another guest picked himself for the list, but his wife interjected, "When was the last time you slept through the night without the help of a little white pill?"

His sheepish reply: "I have to—otherwise I get up every hour to check my BlackBerry."

Amid the laughter, I suddenly felt Jack straighten. "Jim and Linda are happy," he whispered to me for consideration, naming a couple we knew well. We had just attended the husband's sixtieth birthday party, in fact, a celebration right out of a Norman Rockwell painting.

"OK, we have two contenders!" I announced to the table.

And so it went for yet another half hour or more, each couple struggling to come up with a list of a dozen certifiably contented people. Candidates didn't need to be without battle wounds; they didn't even need to be successful by society's standard measures. They just needed to be, we all agreed, at peace with themselves.

So here's the kicker. By the end of the evening, we'd

collectively come up with eleven names. Eleven happy people—out of the hundreds of people we knew from our varied walks of life.

"What a disturbing piece of data," one of our friends summarized as dessert came out and, incongruously, the dance floor started to fill with happy-looking people. "What's going on in this world?"

"Too much pressure," someone said with a shrug. "Technology—it makes everything so fast."

"It's the media," another friend suggested. "You turn on the TV and you see everyone's better house, better car, better job, and better life." He sighed. "The media manufactures envy."

There was a brief lull while we all gazed at each other helplessly.

"Too many decisions, too little time," a voice finally piped up.

"That's it!" I heard myself cry.

Just then, Jack grabbed my hand. "Enough already!" he declared. "I'm officially happy and so's my wife. Come on, everyone, let's dance."

And dance we did until the clock struck midnight and we did what people do at big parties, which is kiss and hug and blither about new beginnings. I'm not complaining; it was a wonderful night. The band was great; my strapless dress stayed up. And when it came time to say goodbye to our friends, we all knew we'd never forget the astonishing conversation we'd shared.

But that night carried extra meaning for me. At the time, I'd shared 10-10-10 with my family and friends; I'd shared it with coworkers and with the readers of my magazine column. But the Happiness List—or, should I say, the difficulty in compiling one—galvanized me to offer 10-10-10 more widely. After all, if complicated decisions were responsible for the scarcity of happiness that we'd hit upon, I had an answer. I knew of an approach to dilemmas that empowered people to create more deliberate, centered, and authentic lives. It wasn't a magic pill or a silver bullet. It required emotional work; it took commitment and candor. But with its simplicity and clarity, 10-10-10 worked.

I'd seen it; I'd lived it. I knew more and more people who were using the idea and seeing their lives transformed.

That night driving home, I resolved to tell their stories.

And so here we are, technically at the completion of that pledge. But this moment hardly feels like an ending to me. If I've learned anything in the process of writing this book, it's that once 10-10-10 is in your life, it's your companion as long as you allow it to work within you and for you.

10-10-10 is still with Antoine, as he continues his life's dream to spread compassion, one welfare client at a time. It's with Ajitha, who recently stopped by my house to tell me how happy her marriage remains. It's with Nancy, who makes decisions every day that allow her to be a wife and daughter in proper measure. It's still with Angela, who recently painted her living room her favorite shade of sunny yellow; and with Maggie, who not long ago welcomed Connor home from three weeks at summer camp, where he had a blast, just like a regular kid.

10-10-10 is of course with me too, helping me live with increasing insight and understanding. It's with my children, as they learn and grow without a magic wand in sight.

In Hawaii, the last thing I ever could have imagined was that sunrise would bring a new idea to change my life. On a strange and wondrous New Year's Eve more than a decade later, I realized that new idea was meant for everyone seeking a way out and a path forward.

If transformation beckons, 10-10-10 is meant for you.

Acknowledgments

An old friend of mine in publishing once told me, "No one ever finishes a book and says, 'Wow, that was easier than I thought.'"

How right she was. Writing a book is not only harder than you imagine, it requires the guidance, patience, and love of more people than you could ever dream of.

I would like to thank those people here.

First, this book would simply not have been possible without the generosity of spirit, humanity, and candor of the many 10-10-10ers who shared their stories with me. I will forever be grateful to the friends, coworkers, and relatives who opened their hearts to describe how 10-10-10 changed their lives, and to the many strangers who became dear friends in doing so.

This book was shaped, nurtured, and improved immeasurably by the superb editorial team at Scribner: Susan Moldow, Roz Lippel, Nan Graham, and Samantha Martin.

The chapter on decision making is in debt to the psychologist and author Daniel Goleman; Nigel Nicholson, a professor of organizational behavior at the London Business School; and Stephen Martin, formerly of the department of philosophy at Tufts University. The chapter on values was enriched by the wisdom of Ken Shigematsu, the pastor of Vancouver's Tenth Avenue Church.

Several friends listened to me think aloud as this book came into being, offering invaluable insights and reading drafts of the manuscript as it went from mind to page: Nancy Bauer, Chris Daly, Liz Feld, Bronwyn Fryer, Sue Herera, Betsy Lack, Joe Tessitore, Marybeth Turner, and Rebecca Wasynczuk. I am especially grateful to Tina Brown for her keen feedback and encouragement, and to Rosanne Badowski for her meticulous copyediting and enduring companionship.

Other friends provided great tidings of comfort and joy along the way: Jeremy Bromberg, Brenda Buttner, Pam Goldman, Susan Krakower, Elaine Langone, Linda Robinson, Linda Tullis, Kim McKown Walters, and Jackie Welch. I thank also Sue Jacobson for sending a constant stream of text messages to keep me centered, and Skye Swett for being my life-support system for the past decade.

My sisters, Elin Kaufman and Della Cushing, blessed me with their unceasing love and support.

My agent Robert Barnett was a steady source of strength and guidance.

I am immensely thankful for the forbearance of the "bosses" at my other jobs as I attended to the work of this one: the *BusinessWeek* editors John Byrne, Ciro Scotti, and Barry Maggs; my good friend and editor at the *New York Times* Syndicate, Michael Oricchio; my editor at *O, The Oprah Magazine,* Mamie Healy; my rock of ages, Janelle Shubert, director of the Center for Women's Leadership at

Babson College; and the living saints at Boston Health Care for the Homeless, Cheryl Kane and Linda Wood-O'Connor.

My children, Roscoe, Sophia, Marcus, and Eve, also endured their share of my distraction with all things 10-10-10, but still managed to love me every day, checking in all the time, being funny and good, and bringing me iced coffee exactly when the iced coffee bell went off in my head. I thank them also for letting me share their stories in these pages without too much hysteria and drama.

Finally, I could not have written this book—full stop—without two people.

When I first met my editorial assistant Megan Slatoff-Burke I knew she was smart, but I had no idea how intensely and wonderfully smart she would be. Nor did I know how much I would come to depend on her cogent push back, deft touch with language, and tireless commitment. Megan read every word in this book—a thousand times—and made every sentence and chapter incalculably better. Thank you, Megan, for everything you have done, and will do, in your brilliant career.

Which leaves my husband, Jack.

There wasn't a day—not an hour—during the writing of this book that Jack was not my best friend, most fanatical booster, and toughest critic. As I traveled around the country to interview 10-10-10 practitioners, Jack would always be the first to hear their stories, usually retold by me over a bad cell phone connection, and his enthusiasm never waned. Later, when I locked myself in a little room to write, Jack abided me like no other. He listened to me ruminate; he encouraged me when it felt too hard. He asked the best questions. And he read everything I wrote, red pen in hand. The truth is, he should have been an editor.

It is the greatest blessing of my life to have him as mine.

P) 1 | 2 | 32 | 72 | 195 | 221

adrenoleukodystrophy P.86

222) dedication – 225

10-13) How To

1. Question needs Answer
2. Data) 134 Stalling
3. Consequences in 10's) 140 Balances
4. Analysis
5. Best Results

P. 75 - 3 paper

Value Prompts

Love + friendships - P. 63 questions / Love 77

WORK - P 102-3) 4 Questions P. 128 - 129 - P. 131 - 132

GROW OR LET GO - P. 107

Leaders) 136-7

138-139) Stalled by old you